PRACTICE SHOWING UP:

A GUIDEBOOK FOR WHITE PEOPLE WORKING FOR RACIAL JUSTICE

By Jardana Peacock

Practice Showing Up: A Guidebook for White People
Working for Racial Justice

 2018

ISBN: 978-0-692-12748-3

Design by Nick Pursche
Cover photo: Amber Cullen, a cultural organizer from
Ohio. Cover photo credit: Brandon Tacadena
Author photo credit: Jacquelyn Tierney
First print edition
First published online in 2016

Please send corrections or typos to
jardana@jardanapeacock.com

ACKNOWLEDGEMENTS AND DEDICATIONS

For all the southern Black and People of Color organizers, Trans and queer magic makers, faith/spiritual leaders and radical healers who have taught me and so many others. You build the world we need, every day.

Please see the resource page at the back to give and support the leadership of People of Color.

To the reader. Thank you for showing up, for being brave, for making mistakes and showing up some more, for hoping and opening your imagination to what could be and what already is.

To my kids, I love you.

This book would not have been possible without the leadership of Susannah Bartlow, who is more than a genius editor. Her attention to cultivating anti-racism as a life path continues to inspire me.

The SURJ community, from the beginning to now, you helped me deepen my analysis of what it means to work with white people. Thank you.

Nick Pursche, whose design work and humility is a blessing.

70% of the proceeds for this book will go to SpiritHouse, Inc. and The Mystic Soul Project.

TABLE OF CONTENTS

Let's Practice Showing Up Together*

In 2018, we experience continued racial injustice, violence and genocide enacted upon Black and Brown bodies. In the US, daily human rights are being threatened under a Trump administration. We are being called to show up differently.

From the powerful visions and leadership of the Movement for Black Lives and Standing Rock, to the lessons we've gleaned from the past movements for change, we know that we make significant impacts towards collective liberation when we focus on strengthening activist and organizer resilience.

All over the world, there are demonstrations, gatherings and actions for Black Lives, immigrants and refugees, calls to end policing and move towards restorative justice are stronger than ever, and more and more white people are coming into consciousness and breaking white silence to end this violence.

And yet, there is urgency that upsets the days and weeks almost every day and week. What are the triage support and structures that need to be embedded in our every day, in our organizing and activism? If this is the state of the world, if this is our reality right now (as my comrade Rusia Mohiuddin recently reminded me) and it's not going to change, if we know that—then how can we change how we show up to meet that reality?

In order for white people to show up, we need practices of healing, spirituality and shared culture to ground us and support us. In July of 2016[1] and again in July of 2017, I put

---

* *Practice Showing Up* was first published online in 2016.

[1] Note on content. Excerpts from "A Way Forward" first appeared in *Heal Myself, Heal the World: Practices for Liberation*, e-book, 2015.

"Sacred Activism: We are the Ones We've Been Waiting For" was originally published in the *Elephant Journal*, February 11, 2017.

"How White Folks can Show up for Racial Justice" was originally published in the *Elephant Journal*, July 17, 2016.

out a call to white folks from a wide range of backgrounds and levels of political engagement and consciousness. I asked them to share stories and practices that support them in showing up for racial justice. In the pages that follow, you will find their writing, meditations, embodied movement, prayer, reflection and other practices to help build our collective resilience.

You can also follow on Facebook and participate at #practiceshowingup. Consider sharing a practice you use in your life and work (a poem, a writing exercise, a meditation or something else) and share a story about being white. Post it to social media using the hashtag #practiceshowingup.

This practice manual is a compilation of some of those practices shared on Facebook, from new and close comrades. Let's use it as a resource to ground our actions, open our meetings and strengthen the resiliency of white people, so we may continue to step into our vulnerable leadership and work for racial justice.

How we are with ourselves and each other is an opportunity to build the world we want to build right now. It is a time for us all to show up: our shared freedom depends on it.

Please share this resource widely.

Let's practice showing up to racial justice together.

Love,

Jardana

A JOURNEY OF BELONGING: EMBODYING WHITE ANTIRACISM AS AN ANCESTRAL PRACTICE

White supremacy, heterosexism, transphobia, ableism, and capitalism are systems of oppression that fog our souls from knowing and believing in ourselves and each other. To love is hard, to heal is hard, to reveal the pain is hard. How little we grow into knowing how to care and hold each other. How much we learn to destroy and critique each other. I show up with a deep desire to build a better world by being the world I need inside and out—and I show up with humility, making mistakes and being duped by a culture of whiteness that never taught me to see. It is through healing and spirituality, through my relationship with God, with the divine, that I return to belonging, return to love.

White supremacy's biggest win is to disconnect people from knowing where we come from. For white folks, there is simultaneously a message that we belong everywhere and yet a disconnection from learning or valuing the roots of where we actually come from. While this is not always true, there is overwhelmingly less emphasis on white people to "know our ancestors" because privilege and power disconnect us from our lineages. One of the shared struggles I hear from white folks in antiracism work is a struggle to define what white culture is and how to create a culture that eradicates the position of racism and supremacy when showing up in a white body.

For white people committed to dismantling internal and external oppression and supremacy systems, the salve for our pain and oppression is to build a culture of belonging, where love is central. Because of the trauma of oppression, this vision seems nearly impossible to operationalize, in part because few of us have experienced white culture as connecting or loving. White supremacy's biggest win is to disconnect us from where we come from and who we come from. However, this journey into healing and building the world we need begins here.

Growing up in Cincinnati, Ohio I understood very early on that we (my immediate family of my Mom, brother and sister) were on our own. My mom was responsible for our survival and no one else. My dad had come in and out of my life since a very early age, although mostly out. He was from Springfield, Ohio from a working class family with a mix of German and English heritage. The story I knew about my father is that he found his father dead, hanging from the basement rafters at a very young age. And while I was young when this story was relayed, it seemed to explain everything about how he was or wasn't a part of the world or our lives. My mother grew up in Bayonne, New Jersey embedded into an Italian family and culture; although my grandmother was technically Dutch and Irish/Welsh/Scots, that culture was dramatically overshadowed by my Grandfather's southern Italian heritage. My grandmother came from a disconnected blood family and welcomed her partner's culture with a zeal that was contagious.

I recall family gatherings almost every Thanksgiving with cousins, aunts, uncles, great aunts and distant cousins with names like Carmen and Toto. Olive colored hands reached and passed antipasto, eggplant Parmesan, and towards the end of an already abundant Italian meal, turkey and cranberry sauce. Through a cacophony of voices and stories, half-started and half-interrupted, everyone talked unapologetically. I still feel the rhythm of those gatherings in my bones. I also recall feeling strangely out of place at the table, as though I was looking into a palindrome, a world where I didn't quite belong even though I wanted to. My great-uncle was a priest and a chef who collected recipes from our lineage like a family tree of tastes and memories. My mother would pull from these book pages and we grew up on homemade tomato sauce and garlicky green beans. Her family were people who seemed mostly to know where they came from. I was of the generation that felt less of that knowing, and yet had direct access to a lineage of people who knew it viscerally. The feeling of strangeness within my own family has haunted me for as long as I can recall.

As I grew older, the visits dwindled and my grandmother got sick and eventually died from cancer. The truth was, she was really the anchor that connected us to a culture of belonging—without her, our family culture became less connected and more whitewashed. My understanding of culture from a very young age was that I was Italian. So, when I had kids who both have red hair, I was a little shocked and interested to know more about where I come from. After getting results back from ancestry dot com, I discovered that the stories of my strong Italian heritage weren't as dominant in my genetic code as I had been taught to believe. I was only 15% Italian. So what else and who else did I come from?

This question has become more and more important over the last decade as I work with other white people and myself through an anti-racism practice and commitment. Understanding who I am and where I come from is a journey of ancestral healing and a map towards belonging to a people and place that I've been largely disconnected from because of white supremacy. My antiracism journey was given language and context when I met Anne Braden, a Louisville organizer who had been working for Civil Rights since the early 50s alongside leaders, such as Ella Baker and Angela Davis. Anne was the first white woman I ever met who asked me to examine my own internalized racism and superiority. She gave me language and a direction for what my whiteness could be in the world, a choice of building the world we need or holding up the supremacy systems that kill us all.

Anne was fierce and clear. White people need to move our bodies towards building a world without oppression and for her that meant organizing other white people, bringing other white people into consciousness and understanding of the deep pain that whiteness upholds for all people. She talked about an inside/outside process that she never coined as spiritual and yet, everything I know about spirituality aligns with the process she mentored me in:

1. Dive deep within and acknowledge the pain.
2. Address the pain through actions and adjustments, inside and out.
3. Practice love, strengthen resiliency and increase your ability to be uncomfortable and strive to embody antiracism in all you do and are. Your soul depends on it.

The years following knowing Anne threw me into a deep internal and external process of organizing for racial justice alongside and with the leadership of mostly Black southern women and other queer white antiracist folks mentored by Anne for many more years than I was.

My first year of graduate school in the Pan-African Studies program was identity shifting. I struggled to fit into the all-Black department, to be "down" enough, to be "antiracist" enough. Little did I know at the time that distancing myself from my whiteness was contributing to maintaining the very oppression I yearned to dismantle. Outside the department and in the community, I was the white girl always calling out other white people, the voice of truth and accountability. However, I wasn't doing what Anne had taught me—to bring more white folks into consciousness. In fact I was pushing most all of the white people away, except those who even more radical than myself.

The truth is I never learned explicitly about loving white folks or even loving myself. I was never taught to learn about or be interested in my ancestry or culture. I learned about love from my spiritual practice and in multiracial organizing. I learned about love off of the picket lines and out of the streets and around the dinner table, at the club with other Pan-African Studies students who taught me how to femme up and show up, I learned about love from the breaking open that happened in SHE, a choreopoetry group I helped found where we dove into our trauma, identities and ancestry through poetry and song. I learned about love in relationships with my Italian family, who connected through shared language and connection, even though I mostly felt like an outsider. I learned about love from loss, the disconnection between my father's family, the disconnection that slowly unraveled from my mother's lines and myself. The disconnection that cratered as I became more politicized and more outwardly queer and didn't fit in as much with my well-meaning liberal immediate and right-leaning extended family.

Building a culture of belonging, care and love is at the very center of dismantling white supremacy culture. If we're not practicing now inside our communities, groups and cultures what we want in the world, we will not create the world we need. When we skip over the practice, we miss practicing equity and social justice in how we are together. Without that we are not going to survive. This is spiritual work. This is the work of antiracism. When we break open our identities, supremacy systems, we reveal a wound and we must be the salve for each other. To be vulnerable, to admit our mistakes, to see each other and love on each other—this is how we will build a better world this is how we learn to belong to each other. This work is hard; it's trauma work. It's returning to our humanity when we work for antiracism and we must do that in our relationships with each other and across race, in organizations, and internally too if we are to actualize liberation.

Antiracism is a journey of returning to what was lost for all us, although differently lost and experienced depending on our containers. Antiracism is a journey in, a path to heal ancestral disconnection and an opportunity to build love, belonging and step into the imagination of a different world. One where we return to humanness, of connection and heal disconnection. We must belong, if we are to ever understand why the journey matters.

SACRED ACTIVISM: WE ARE THE ONES WE'VE BEEN WAITING FOR

We are in heavy times. Every day, I hear from activists on the front lines: Folks are weary. Changemakers have been mired in a veil of depression and heaviness since the election of he-who-shall-not-be-named.

It's in the air and seeping into our bodies and souls, toxic particles of hopelessness and defeat. Our defenses are reaction, urgency, and self- and public critique.

Where to begin, when there is so much to begin? How to rise, when there is so much that needs resisting? How to move, when we are so weary?

Our souls beg for nourishment, and our human community desperately desires connection.

And this undernourishment, this disconnection is the very thing we are most scared of. This is one of the reasons we are in a tailspin of doubt, shame and fear.

The voices that tell us we have failed as a radical, progressive and even liberal left are loud. We are quick to accept this nugget, because it's delivered straight from the jaws of white supremacy and capitalism itself. The very systems that we live inside of and replicate unknowingly when we allow these voices to dominate our actions, spirits and hearts.

To face how systems of oppression show up inside of us would be to recognize the Trump supporter within us.

A few months ago, on the crowded steps of the Muhammad Ali Center in Louisville, Kentucky, people chanted: "No hate, no fear, refugees are welcome here." Under the artificial glow of yellow streetlights and through the grey smoke of our chanting breath, a small group of 10 white supremacists faintly heckled hate as they waved the United States flag. The crowd of thousands shifted from their focused chanting to address the small group: "You are not welcome here." Someone shouted at them. You could feel the collective body ignite, alive with triggers and trauma as the reaction of disdain and hate grew for the supremacists, taking us off course.

And I felt deeply in my body how this reaction stems from a place of deep pain within us. A feeling that maybe, as activists, especially white activists, we don't belong here, either. Because we aren't active enough, or vocal enough, or radical enough. Or enough.

Here, in this moment of division, inside and out, white supremacy wins again. We mirror each other.

The hate and pain of this nation do not occupy the white supremacists and racists alone; it lives within each of us. And some aspect of this trauma lives in all of us.

When we divide ourselves from each other, we feed the chasm on which systems of oppression thrive. Many white folks will say: "But I am not racist. But I am not them."

No, and yes.

That Kentucky winter night of the demonstration, I was

reminded of what my friend and colleague Ebony Noelle Golden[2], a cultural organizer, recently wrote:

> "A protest is a collective public ritual, not a party or a parade. It's a serious matter of energetic/spiritual/creative exchange. Our ancestors show up, guides show up, other forces show up. Don't go out in the streets un-protected, spiritually. This is spiritual. If you are not physically, spiritually, and emotionally ready for battle, stay home and take care."

As I stood on those concrete steps and the crowd leaned toward addressing the hecklers, I rocked my baby and started to sing, "We are the ones we've been waiting for," a song written by Sweet Honey In the Rock that I learned at the Highlander Center. I imagined a beam of light running from my heart to the white supremacists and holding all of us in its blaze, a practice similar to ones found in my Tantric yoga practice and tonglen from Buddhism.

It is a spiritual imperative for our times to resist siloing ourselves from each other, disconnecting, and moving too quickly from the pain to the relief. This is part of the reason we are in this political climate to begin with. I know that the people standing across the street on a foundation of hate are there because they are in pain too; they are in pain from inner disconnection. I know this, because I know this pain.

This pain arises within us, triggered by reminders of our links to colonization, hate and violence from our ancestors, and from our present reality. One solution is to strengthen our resiliency by equipping ourselves with holistic practices, seeking spiritual grounding and ceremony, and facing the mirrors of hate and violence outside and within us to

---

[2] Find more about Ebony's work here: https://bettysdaughterarts.com

love people into connection with each other and the earth. We must love ourselves in our mistakes and flaws.

We are good at feeding the voices of doubt and pain inside. This unprocessed pain is oppression; we carry it within our bodies and psyches and spirits and pass it on through generations. Supremacy systems want us to be ill-equipped to feel liberation, courage, hope and love. When we avoid the oppression, the pain and trauma, then we remain ill-equipped to step into that place of liberation. We show up as less of who we are when self-doubt, shame and guilt freeze us in a constant criticizing internal dialogue.

It's time to go deeper into the oppression inside and heal, so we can show up as the leaders the world needs us to be.

Knitting this divide is an internal process, but it is also a spiritual one. How can we resist in ways that include our bodies and communities? How can we resist in ways that weave in more silliness and play? How can we resist in ways that harness love? The kind of love that opens, invites, forgives, and is inevitably more powerful because it allows us to hold the pain simultaneously with the loving. What if we showed up to everything as a reverent act, a sacred ceremony of connection, both with ourselves and with others? What if we tempered the urge to critique or separate ourselves from each other, and instead softened into the place that exists within us that is the same?

What if, as black feminist writer and organizer June Jordan said, we are the ones we've been waiting for, exactly as we are?

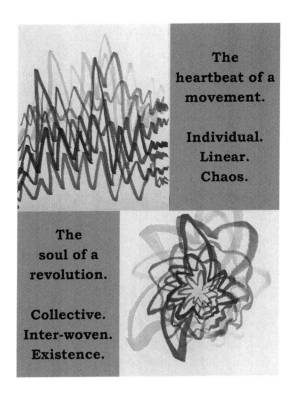

The
heartbeat of a
movement.

Individual.
Linear.
Chaos.

The
soul of a
revolution.

Collective.
Inter-woven.
Existence.

Rebecca Frederick

America 2017: A time of deep resistance. A resistance that started long before us. That we carry now for those after us. We find ourselves in a time that calls us all to move in ways unknown to us. Called to move with an urgency those of us with deep privilege do not understand because survival has come easier for us. We should move with caution when holding that urgent energy, which carries the life of many. If we move forward in individual ways to maintain our individual status quo we will never interact with those who are different than us to create real change that keeps the center held sacred for those deepest in the margins. We have to find a way to hold our urgent energy together so we can create that sacred space at the center of our change for people of color who are also women, trans folks, queer, poor, sex workers, and so many more. Can we take a collective breath and move in ways that weave our individual beings into a collective community that holds justice, dignity and humanity at the center?

PRACTICES FROM WHITE PEOPLE SHOWING UP

OPENING PRACTICE

Jes Kelley, North Carolina

In this moment, what is surfacing on the topic of showing up for racial justice as a white person is this...

I bring my heart. I find that there is slightly little less room for ego when the heart is leading. On some days my heart breaks a thousand times at how terrible and beautiful the world is; this keeps me present and open. On some days my heart is shielded behind ribs and sternum feeling tenacious and solid. These different modes, and the spaces between them increase my resiliency, my capacity for joy and for grief.

I understand racial justice to be a spiritual practice, a healing practice, a heart practice. The keyword being practice. To me, anti-racism at its root is a practice of reconnecting to self and to others. The primary strategy that guilt, shame and fear have in common is to generate disconnection and isolation. Therefore, I understand that our primary strategy has to be to generate connection through relationships and action. It is not possible to solely think our way out of white supremacy, we must also feel our way out. Staying in my heart and in connection with beloved community as much as possible helps me to practice doing this imperfectly everyday.

EMBODIED PRACTICES

Susannah Bartlow, Tennessee

Practice Showing up for Racial Justice: Body Awareness

This practice will get you out of your head and into your body in times of stress and overwhelm. This technique is passed down from Rusia Mohiuddin and rev. angel Kyodo williams, from the Oppression in the Soma/Practicing Justice retreat.

As a white person from an academic family, one of the things I learned in difficult, overwhelming, painful, or stressful—sometimes even joyful—situations was to be brain-centered and analyze what was happening, often at the expense of other parts of my body. I didn't learn as much how to integrate my language or my analysis with the environment, but instead conditioned myself to be a brain on top of a spine-pole.

So, it's been helpful to have practices that bring me back home to body awareness. Yoga, running, hiking, music, art, dancing, and meditation have all been resources at different times. This short, simple, small practice has also become a powerful habit. I use it in meetings, in the middle of a crowded room—really anywhere that I notice myself reverting to dissociation.

1. **Take your index finger and middle finger together and rub, press or tap on the center of your chest, close to your heart, between your breastbone.** This simple habit works anywhere and is effective even without meditation or anything leading up to it—just a bit of pressure right at the divot in your breastplate, anywhere from 2-4 inches below your clavicle. If you're not sure where to press, begin at the base of your throat, and draw your fingers down slowly until you notice a shift in your energy, breathing, or awareness. You can pause here if that's satisfying.

2. **If you want to keep going, close your eyes, focus on your breathing, and take a long exhale.** This can help bring awareness into your belly/midsection. You then have two points of contact with your body—heart and belly. The exhale can help you draw awareness out to the other forms of intelligence and presence you have in the world.

3. **Close by pressing or resting your hand over your heart.** This closes the practice sweetly. It also can soothe a tendency to take hostility inward instead of expelling it outward; as a white person, especially if I'm in my guilt matrix, I end up pressing really hard with a self-aggressive gesture and an internalized message of "you better be present for this". But that anger is really directed at the system that's harming people and pressing hard against myself changes nothing. So I lighten or loosen my press, hold hand over heart, and breathe.

With this short practice, I'm less hyperstimulated, less in my head, and more likely to take reasonable risks that come from heart and gut as well as mind. The goal for me is to do things that are of benefit to the Movement for Black Lives and to myself becoming more whole. May this practice be of benefit.

Mike Clawson, Texas

The Spiritual Practice of Biting My Tongue

Most of the time, I am a fairly introverted person... *except* when I get excited about an intellectual discussion. Then I can tend to take over, rambling on and dominating a conversation with my own perspective and ideas.

I remember once in college when a friend, a young woman, literally left the room crying because I was so oblivious to the ways I was talking over her and failing to make space for her point of view.

After graduation, I became a youth pastor and slowly, gradually began to learn the subtle art of actually listening to the people sitting across from me. Pastoral ministry has a way of demanding that. I think I got better at it. At least, fewer people left the room crying when they came to talk to me.

I also started noticing the ways certain types of people, usually women or persons of color, tended to get talked over more often by people like me, i.e. assertive white males. I remember one group I was in, a discussion group for pastors and lay leaders, where the only people who ever really talked were the older white male pastor types, while the women could almost never get a word in edgewise. Or if they did begin to speak, one of the white alpha pastor guys would soon interject and end up co-opting her point.

I realize this is a common experience for most women, but it was a new revelation for me at the time.

It was then that I developed what I call "the spiritual practice of biting my tongue." I mean this quite literally. When I found myself in such situations, I would actually begin to bite the sides of my tongue whenever I felt an urge to interrupt or talk-over a woman, person of color, or anyone else in the group who seemed shut-out by the more conversationally aggressive participants like myself. Biting my tongue was a way to remind myself to shut up, stop interrupting, and really listen to those I needed to hear most – to those whose voices are typically marginalized or dismissed in our society and whose experiences are so different than my own as a middle-class, cis-het, white male. I needed that embodied, physical practice – an actual painful bite, not just a gentle mental reminder – to disrupt the assumption of privilege and dominance that I had previously operated with.

It may seem like a simple or silly thing, but this practice has proved invaluable to me in the years since...

By biting my tongue, I was able to hear the experiences of all the women who were being crowded out of my conversations.

By biting my tongue, I was able to hear my LGBTQ+ friends when they told me that their sexual orientation was not just a "sinful" choice they were making, but was in fact an integral part of who they are.

By biting my tongue, I was able to hear the voices of the working classes when they insisted that our economic system might be working for the 1%, but it wasn't working for them.

By biting my tongue, I was able to hear my Black brothers and sisters when they cried out against the ongoing violence and discrimination being perpetrated against them and instead declared that Black lives do matter.

Through the spiritual practice of biting my tongue... and then really listening to those with less power and privilege than myself, I was able to become a better ally, a better activist, and a better human being. I would recommend the practice to anyone with a similar need to listen better and learn more.

Carol J Kraemer, Kentucky

Circle of Love (a song)[3]
by Carol J Kraemer 1/19/17
Translation by Karina Barillas and Luis DeLeon

If they come for my Muslim neighbor
They'll have to come through me
If they come for any one of us
we'll make a circle of love for all to see

If they come for my:
~Black brother
~immigrant sister
~poor comrade
~our union workers

~differently abled
~Queer and Trans siblings
~Native Family
~Our sisters' right to choose
~Our Mother Earth
~Beloved Community

Si vienen por mí vecino musulmán
Tendrán que pasar por mí
Si vienen por nosotros
Haremos círculo de amor

Hermano Negro
Hermana Inmigrante
Compañero pobre
Nuestras sindicalistas
Los discapacitados
Los y las transgénero
Los indígenas
Nuestros derechos reproductivos
Tierra Madre
Comunidad amada

---

3   Video Facebook link to a portion of the song from Carla Wallace's Birthday party. Singers/
    players: Luis DeLeon, Cynthia Fletcher, Andrew Newton and Carol at Center for African
    American Heritage, March 3, 2017. (https://www.facebook.com/bethbissmeyer/videos/
    923337867233/)

Maggie MacLeod, North Carolina

I've been engaging in issues of racial justice for years. One of the pitfalls of being a white person committed to this work has been my ego. With terms like "wokeness" becoming popular, it's easy to compliment myself or ourselves, but I consistently learn that I'm not perfect, I do not know everything, and I need to defer to friends who are living experiences of injustice that I don't and won't understand. As a recovering perfectionist, I'm beginning to find the beauty in that surrender: it's wonderful that I learn something every day, and that my views are challenged by reading an article or talking to someone about a new idea. Humility, bravery, accountability - these require connection to myself and to community.

I extend this 30 minute, slower-paced, trauma-informed practice to you. Our humility does not mean we don't tend to our own wounds. I offer many options, and gently invite you to check in with your body and breath so we white folks can continue showing up in the world for racial justice.

Trauma-Informed Yoga Practice Sequence

- *Comfortable seat*
  Such as easy seat or kneeling. Eyes open or closed. Hands may be on your lap or one on belly and one on chest. A few moments of aware breathing through nose or mouth.
- *Mindful attention*
  To where body is at beginning of practice
- *Belly breathing / 3 part breath for 3 breaths*
- *Neck rolls*
- *Shoulder rolls*

- *Eagle arms on the right side*
  Optional to have something to hold on to between the hands
  - *Cat and cow with arms as is*
    Could be in easy sitting or on knees
- *Eagle arms on the left side*
  - *Cat and cow with arms as is*
    Could be in easy sitting or on knees
- *Tabletop*
- *Cat and Cow*
- *Child's pose with arms extended*
- *Downward facing dog*
- *Right side low lunge*
  With back knee on the ground or lifted, hands on the ground framing the foot, or bring the hands onto the knee balancing
- *Child's pose or Downward Dog*
- *Left side low lunge*
  With back knee on the ground or lifted, hands on the ground framing the foot, or bring the hands onto the knee balancing
- *Child's pose or Downward Dog*
- *Bridge*
  Option to clasp hands underneath the body, 1-2 times
- *Knees into chest*
  Rock knees side to side or in a circle
- *Figure 4 on L and R*
- *Extend legs*
- *Supine twist to the R*
- *Supine twist to the L*
- *Savasana*
  Any position you find comfortable - such as lying on your back, on your side, or standing
- If on the floor, introduce some gentle movement, inhale, roll over onto the side and come up to seated for closing

Yoga Practice: https://soundcloud.com/user-954528374/practice-showing-up-maggie

The Role of Love in Antiracism

I opened my arms. I stretched my collar bone up towards the sky and softened my knees, "I'm just going to love everyone, is what I tell myself when I start to tighten up or disengage." The white women standing around after the toddler music class began to laugh. They listened closely as I shared my vulnerable presence practice (see below).

In my time on the road and connecting with people across the world, I've heard a lot of the same issues, desires and needs from folks.

People desire connection, they are hungry for a community to belong to and white people feel a deep pain around being white.

White folks struggle to connect with other white folks, especially in antiracism work, and in social justice work. There is incredible competition, one upping, critique and divide and conquer, even in social justice spaces.

Do you feel me?

What is this about?

White supremacy.

White supremacy wins when we are isolated, divided and disconnected from our bodies and from each other.

What would it mean to create welcoming community in our movements for change? What would it mean to choose love as the antidote for the ways that internalized and interpersonal white supremacy shows up in our change making spaces?

These are questions I'm sitting with too.

As we move forward with a desire to make change inside and out, here are a few guidelines I'm carrying with me. Perhaps they are useful for you too:

1. How do I best serve? What is my work, what are my leverage points, spheres of influence and deepest passions and how can they be used to catalyze change inside and out?

2. Where do I feel uncomfortable or resistant and why? And, how can I deepen into this place to learn more about myself and explore places to heal, and to open me to human connection and to vulnerability?

3. How can I be more accountable? What are the ways that I participate in status quo behavior? How can I deepen my connections with folks across difference (political and socio-economic) and more intentionally build with colleagues and comrades?

4. Am I listening in to spirit or being led by ego/white supremacy? This is a hard one for us white folks. However, because I know that when I show up to practice, relationships and deeply dive into history/ learning that I am more connected to spirit and love, then it's my responsibility to maintain these aspects of life as the very way I will be part of dismantling white supremacy inside and out.

5. Am I showing up to this moment as though it is sacred? This one has been a bit of an affirmation for me lately. Every interaction is an opportunity to tap intothe divinity within and around me. How am I showing up to that?

6. What am I a part of building and how am I tapping into the imagination to do that? We often get stuck in patterns and habits that keep us in a rut. I see this so much in the social justice movement. Lately I am asking myself, is this a strategy or action that will yield the desired result or is there another way we haven't considered?

7. How am I using my whiteness to dismantle supremacy systems and how am I ignoring my whiteness and maintaining systems of oppression? I must constantly consider, as a white woman, how am I part of dismantling and how am I part of maintaining systems of oppression. White supremacy runs deep and if I am not in accountable relationship with others and with spirit, it is easy to fall into privilege and maintain supremacy systems. Some actions I'm taking around this include participating in an antiracist training (you can never do this enough), building in vulnerable relationships and diving deep into discomfort as an exploration of healing and connection.

8. How am I opening my heart, being vulnerable and connecting to others and myself in healing and love? This brings us back to the vulnerable presence practice I opened up with. I'd like to share that now for you to try on.

I know that white supremacy wants to disconnect me from my body and from my heart. When I feel discomfort rising, when I feel social anxiety setting in and especially when I am around a lot of people I do not know, I engage in the following practice.

This is a practice I have learned from too many people to name. I honor my movement mentors, my spiritual teachers, Spirit and my community by sharing this with you.

Breathe. Observe the ways your body is tightening and the ways it is open.

Breathe into your heart. Imagine your heart is opening up like a flower, or expanding like the ocean (find an image that works). Observe the tenderness or resistance as you breathe your heart open.

Tell yourself: "I love you, I love you, I love you." Say this to yourself. I often hold my hand at my heart as a comforting gesture. Then, "I love you, I love you, I love you" to everyone around you. As you show up in spaces of discomfort, remind yourself that you are love and your role is to connect with love.

Observe your body. Breathe.

We've got to love ourselves and each other more open. For more on why this is important for activists, read *Love Everyone: A Guide for Spiritual Activists* by Sharon Salzberg and Rev. angel Kyodo williams.[4]

This life is a beautiful opportunity to connect with each other, ourselves and the natural world. We must do the deep work of healing, learning and examining the ways internalized oppression shows up and engage in the work of showing up to others and ourselves with compassionate understanding.

We all hold varying levels of pain within us.

Love is not easy; it is one of the most challenging actions I've personally engaged in.

---

4   https://www.lionsroar.com/love-everyone-a-guide-for-spiritual-activists/

The greatest win for supremacy systems was to create divisions between us and embed internalized doubt within us. This internalized doubt disconnects us from the ability to easily access healing and to trust our inner wisdom.

This history cannot be undone quickly. It cannot be undone through an intellectual process alone. It is felt, in the body, in the pain and in the reconnection to the truth of our interconnected humanity.

Willa Conway, California and kate poole, Maryland

Rituals and Practices for Giving

Kate Poole and I are committed to racial and economic justice, freedom, liberation, unrestricted joy, creativity, and wildness. We know that our movement requires us to show up fully, consistently, and with humility, love, and rigor. We are also white and wealthy and believe in and are in practice around redistributing our financial resources to movement work for our collective liberation.

In addition to our organizing and resource mobilization work, we have each found body-based practices that keep us grounded, curious, and connected both necessary and important. The movement work we are called to takes our whole selves. When we're working on systemic change, we need to address our bodies as systems that reflect the imbalances and injustices of the world. We can't expect to be healthy in a polluted system so these practices can help us get clear on all that we are working with as we transform ourselves and our communities.

In a time filled with radical vision, movement building, deportations, violence, monstrous policy changes, and horrible Twitter feeds, we offer this work as a tool to push through the stories that keep us from being bold and balanced. We need to mobilize resources and invest in the long haul. We need to build together, personally and collectively, a liberatory future. Please join us!

You can reach out to us and stay connected through: bit.ly/kateandwilla

We are working with and inspired by:

- adrienne maree brown & emergent strategy:
  https://www.alliedmedia.org/esii
- cooperation jackson: http://www.cooperationjackson.org
- Generative Somatics: http://www.generativesomatics.org
- Liberatory Leadership Project and Liberation School:
  http://www.liberatoryleadership.org
- movement generation: http://movementgeneration.org
- Movement netlab: https://movementnetlab.org
- Resource Generation: https://resourcegeneration.org
- Solidaire Network: https://solidairenetwork.org
- Thousand Currents: https://thousandcurrents.org

rituals and practices for giving

start with

getting grounded
sending roots down

back to basics
land water
sleep
eat
movement
take a walk

and then

getting clear around yes
or no

make your giving plan
(self-forgiveness)

in your process
set limits to do grounding exercise
eat movement

journaling

how does this piece fit into the whole
why does this matter for me - its bigger than us

we will shift
wealth and power

△ we need courage to take bold action △

you can strengthen and ground
your giving by adding ritual
to your check-writing + money-sending
set an altar, get dressed up
light a candle, invite your ancestors
inside your teachers in, pick flowers, put on a wig,
pull out photo of the organization & people
you're moving money to, pull out special
objects like keys, letters, stones, tokens
say a prayer prayer

we learn by doing, the most important
thing is building relationships with
the people you're giving to, and
that's a long term promise

put a date on your calendar
to take a talk, drink tea and
reflect on your giving

stay connected at bit.ly/Kate and willa

Willa Conway and kate poole

WRITING & REFLECTIVE PRACTICES

Will Brummett, Tennessee

In the face of increased violence, I have struggled recently around how to show up on social media. The practice I offer you is for when questions or blocks arise for you too. This is how I moved through the fear of posting to social media and how I got to the root of my block.

For me, developing and reacting on a question I was struggling with was key towards uncovering my block.

"Why am I so hesitant to post on social media right now?" I then meditated on it for seven minutes and free-wrote for about ten minutes. It was raw and not pretty, but it forced me to come to terms with why I was struggling. The ugly truth is my privilege and fear have allowed me countless times to create Facebook statuses more than I ever created action in these times when I am called to do more. I offer the below reflection for any fellow white people who may be feeling the same and to challenge us to move from collective conversation on Facebook to actual collective liberation efforts.

White Status Symbol: My Inadequate, Repeated Response to Tragedy by Will Brummett

What should be the status I post?
Why is that almost always my first question
As part of this accepted, social ritual to reconcile others' demise

Without having to revolutionize my own lifestyle
My silence pleads the 5th
Unwilling to speak about my crime of continued inaction
Unable to claim anything else.

I've never known a status to save a soul
Or a conversation thread to weave people together
the words I post simply distract from the background
   behind it; a landscape of whiteness

That keeps you scrolling down
But never standing up.
This is for white 'allies' like me
Who shift from disbelief to shame
From shame to guilt
From guilt to anger
From anger to analyzing
From analyzing to attributing the problem to
people and systems who we clarify 'are not like us.'
They are just our blood family.
But when you live comfortably in the towers of white
   supremacy it does not matter if you did not intend
   to build it

It matters that you've stayed.
Do not only post statuses that free us from guilt
Post bail for those who sat in a street instead of their
office chair
Do not simply like articles that you will never fully read
Instead, read the eyes of the community around you
See if there is something you can learn from them.
Do not share this post because it is easy
share your heart, your anger, your courage, your
   repentance because it is hard.
And then listen.
Because words we post are not the true statuses of
   our lives
The lives we live show the real status of our collective
humanity. 'Like it' or not.

Kate Cavanagh, New York

Yesterday I paused and asked myself, "Why do Black Lives Matter to me?" Immediately a lived experience that I only shared with a few close friends came to my mind so I wrote a poem about it to share publicly here with family and friends. White people—can you do the same and post? This is one of my practices to process and heal. What are yours? Our collective healing and love, breaking the silence will change us and change this cycle of violence. Join me.

Why Black Lives Matter to Me by Kate Cavanagh

Walking down the street
Outside of the elementary school
I worked at
A scene I see all too often
Living in a neighborhood
That is Latino, Middle Eastern and Asian
White NYPD officer pushing a Latino boy
He was no more than 13 years old
I freeze
I walk closer
I work up my courage
The officer sees me watching.
"What do you want?" he barks at me.
"Hi officer, I work at the school right here.
Is there anything I can do?"
I use my best, friendly white lady voice.
"Do you know his name?" he glares
"No, but I am sure I have seen him before." I smile.
"You don't know him. Keep walking." His hatred is
    palpable.
"I think I will stand right here until he is free to go. Is
    he free to go?" I ask innocently.
"What the fuck is wrong with you?" he spits.

"Excuse me?" I stutter.

"You heard me... keep walking." He motions with his head.

"I'm a teacher here and I just want to make sure all of our students are safe. Is he in some kind of trouble?"

The officer yells, "GET THE FUCK OUT OF HERE! I WILL ARREST YOU RIGHT NOW. DO YOU WANT TO GET ARRESTED?

GET THE FUCK OUT OF HERE!"

I breathe deep and ground.

I don't move.

He grabs the child by the shoulder and brings him across the street

Into moving traffic.

"DON'T FUCKING FOLLOW ME I WILL FUCKING ARREST YOU. I WILL ARREST YOU RIGHT NOW. KEEP FUCKING WALKING. THAT'S RIGHT. KEEP FUCKING WALKING."

He puts his hand on his holster touching his gun making sure that I can see it.

I think about my child (because then it was only one).

I actually had time to think.

I actually got to choose.

My skin color accorded me that.

The young boy says, "It's OK Miss...."

Except it's not ok... what is happening is not ok

I am alone I think... no one is here to videotape...

I don't have a badge number I think....

I can't call 911 on a cop I panic....

I don't want to get shot today....

I don't want to get beat down to the ground today.

Headlines flash through my head.

Would they lie about me saying I assaulted the officer or something?

Would my family believe the lies?

My family loves police officers.

My family trusts police officers
My family might believe this cop over me
Because he has taken an oath to "serve and protect"
My family might just believe the police officer
Because I should have "minded my own business"
And kept silent like a good white person should.
My white silence is violence.
I cried. I don't know what happened to that boy.
I walked away.
I don't know what happened to that boy.
My white mind says, "Oh nothing... the cop let him
    go of course after roughing him up a little." I don't
    know that.
That's actually not how it always goes.
I get off with a warning, a threat because I am white.
He might be dead.
He might have been beaten.
He might have been detained.
He might have been fined.
I am alive.
I got to walk away.
I think that's actually fucked up
Because my partner
My partner's family
My friends
My coworkers
My neighbors
Who are black and brown
Don't get to walk away
And I've seen it first hand
It's not a few bad apples
It is the whole damn system.
It is the whole damn system.
That is why Black Lives Matter to me.

Rev. Dr. Michelle Walsh, Massachusetts

I lived and ministered in an urban community of color for nearly two decades, the longest part of which was as a lay community minister rather than clergy. That period of my life was both my most rewarding and growth-filled and also my most challenging emotionally and spiritually. I grew up white working class in mostly rural areas of Ohio, with little exposure to people of races different from myself. I understood more about class than about race when I first embarked by quirks of fate and history in becoming responsible for an urban youth ministry program – and initially Zen Buddhist mindfulness practices in Thich Nhat Hanh's tradition were important in sustaining me.

However, I quickly learned that perseverance and joy in the learning through the challenges, joy in the perseverance and the "aha" moments that accompany a process of becoming "woke" to more and more levels of awareness, are key to the practice.

Risking Encounter – Risking Affirmation – Risking Change

Here is a true story from early in my ministry as an example of an "aha" moment that led to a deeper spiritual awakening.

Take a moment to consider: *As white people, what spiritually moves each of us to risk being engaged in such encounters – to have our consciousness raised and to connect and take action across social boundaries?*

Now free write for 5-10 minutes.

Here's the story: One Thursday night in 2005, I had an opportunity to be a participant-observer with a group of Boston urban teens, primarily African American, in an exercise called

"Community Build." I was not familiar with it, but my general rule-of-thumb for oppression awareness exercises is to go with the flow of my feelings and analyze later. We were split into four communities: chocolate, mint, strawberry and vanilla. Each group was sent to taped off areas on the floor which were next to each other and they were given an envelope filled with rules and some play money. We were told that each group had to follow the rules and build the best community they could with the resources they were given.

Now, I'm a really "good" white working class kid at heart in how I was raised, and I know how to follow the rules to get to the stated goal. These rules included that we could not set foot in anyone's else's community, we had to purchase building permits for what we wanted in our community, and we needed to get a police officer to escort one of us outside our community to purchase the building permit. I quickly set to work empowering the kids in my mint community to make purchase decisions with the very nice sum of money we seemed to have. I was aware that the chocolate community to our left was having a lot of fun and seemed to be able to buy a lot more things than us mints, and I also was vaguely aware that there was some discontent and complaints brewing in the strawberry and vanilla communities to my right, but I stayed pretty focused on the goal of getting our comfortable mint community set up. At one point, my community member Keith accidentally stepped into the chocolate community and almost got arrested, but the police officer let him go when I vouched for him.

Then suddenly, things began to get louder in the vanilla community – which when I paused to really look at it appeared to be seriously crowded from having very little space and there was commotion over the police trying to reduce their space even further with tape. Some type of civil disobedience was taking place as I observed the white adult member, Bruce (a fellow ministry staff member), being physically carried off to jail by the police. From jail, Bruce began to sing "We shall overcome!" Rowdiness increased in the vanilla community and one of their members, Janee, stepped into our mint community. I very loudly and gamely with humor in following the rules began to call for the police to arrest her and she rather vigorously began to resist arrest. At that point, more seriously, I became afraid that Janee or the police officer might get hurt, so I said to Janee: "Janee, calm down. It's OK. You need to follow the rules. You need to go to jail." Janee looked at me with these very wide and idealistic eyes and said, "No! Bruce said we need to stick together!"

Wow! Amazed "aha" moment. What was I saying to her?? In that moment of powerful connection - of revelation and conversion - I jumped the line from my mint community into the vanilla community. I don't know who was more shocked - the vanilla community or my own mint community! Calls of "traitor," "traitor" followed in my wake - and no one followed me over. I would love to report that I then inspired others to join me in nonviolent resistance to the real poverty I found in the vanilla community. But no, I yielded to the impulse to try to steal mint's store with Janee. After that, we were left with a humorous small riot with the police.

Yet all in all, something in this metaphorical game became very real to me about the rigid social boundaries we create and the institutional mechanism through which we maintain them. It took Janee looking me directly in the eye and speaking with fierce idealism and outrage for her to be real to me and to get me to wake up and make a radical change – and even then the path to spiritual unity and knowledge of how to collectively challenge the structures effectively, creatively, and with moral authority were not automatic. Yet first had to come the direct encounter with the full personhood of another resisting my attempt to minimize or silence – and my willingness to risk that encounter and respond with an affirmation.

Take a moment to consider: *What does it take and will it take for you?*

Now free write for 5-10 minutes.

Harley Meyer, Vermont

Below is a draft of a writing workshop specifically for white people to practice breaking silence around racism, process white supremacy and police brutality against Black people emotionally/poetically in a contained space, and make creative commitments to Black Lives Matter. This draft contains a lot of material, so please choose the practices and prompts that will work best for your setting and your group. With love and gratitude to cultural workers of color who move the earth to do amazing work every day. With love and thanks to Favor Ellis and Beth Pecoraro for their feedback on this workshop.

Consider making the workshop available for a suggested donation to Black Lives Matter.

Part 1:
1. Create the space that you feel will be most supportive for the workshop and participants. This could mean calling in sacred space, creating an altar, or simply lighting a candle. Describe the goal and intention of the workshop. All feelings are welcome, all levels of embodiment/disembodiment welcome.

2. Brief grounding exercise:
   a. Invite everyone to plant their feet and/or feel their sit bones/another body part rooted into the earth through gravity. Imagine vibrant red roots reaching down from your body into the earth. Imagine the roots hugging you into the earth, reassuring, safe, and nurturing.

3. Free write (7 min)

4. Write a list of 5 things that brought you here today, and then write one clear intention for our time together.

5. When Sandra Bland was killed, I felt... (12 min)

6. When Alton Sterling was killed, I felt... (12 min)

7. When Philando Castile was killed, I felt.... (12 min)

8. When Black lives are harmed or destroyed, I feel... (12 min)

9. Take a breath. Please notice a place in your body that is feeling a lot of intensity right now (you can put a hand on it, breath into it, or visualize it from a distance). Write what that place would like to say right now. Consider it may have a voice different than your own. (7 min)

10. Paint a mural of your grief, sadness and numbness. Tell me everything about it as you paint it, including where you are painting it. (7 min)

11. Tell me everything you know about anger.

12. Write a letter to Shame and Silence. This may be the first time you are speaking directly to them. Remind them when you first met. What would you like to say to them?

Take a quick break. Invite the group to breathe, reconnect with their big red roots, and do a quick body scan (upclose scan or far-away imaginary scan).

Part 2:
Resource Mapping
13. Make a list of your deep, true, human gifts and talents.

14. Make a list of the resources and communities you are connected to.

15. Pass around a list of things white people can do to support Black Lives Matter* (there are several good ones out there – check out SURJ for resources). Pick three that sing to you, challenge you, grab your eye or your heart.

16. Draw some connections, literally, with circles and lines on the paper. How can you connect what you already have with these action steps?

17. If you're comfortable, find a partner and share your lists. Make sure to discuss at least one connection that you feel is hot, exciting, scary, or seemingly impossible.

Part 3:

Closing

18. Write a love letter to yourself. Check in with the intention you set at the beginning, and let your love letter lean into it. (7 min)

19. Write one new intention for when you put down your pen and walk out of this room.

20. Breathe together, thank everyone for being here.

21. Provide information about next steps, invite folks to stay and talk in detail about their resource map, include upcoming events/actions in your area, and connect them to local Showing Up for Racial Justice (SURJ) chapters and other organizations working to support Black Lives Matter.*

*Resources

How Writers Can Join the Fight Against Police Violence (https://docs.google.com/document/d/12Us3brfEhKS FJ34HDF6d50WyLRsLHWAPPT0fcJ2VWUI/edit)

26 Ways to be in Struggle Beyond the Streets (https://issuu.com/nlc.sf.2014/docs/beyondthestreets_final)

In Memoriam of Philando Castile (*http://www.pollenmidwest.org/stories/in-memoriam-of-philando-castile/*)

Abraham Lateiner, Massachusetts

A practice I often use is what I call the "superhero power practice." The white savior mentality is a well known issue, where white people come in and "save the day." In part this savior mindset exists because of a white superiority complex. Many white folks are used to having power, and we bring that expectation into racial justice spaces. This causes us to act out of ego instead of a commitment to collective liberation.

For me, I know that centering my ego as a white person is problematic, but that doesn't actually stop me from doing it. One thing I can do to control the pull of ego is to speak it aloud and laugh with self-compassion and humility.

Leading with that kind of vulnerability reduces any sense of competition I have with other white people. When I am willing to do the work of looking deeply into the mirror as a white person, then I am able to work with what I see.

If I can't face that mirror, laugh tenderly at my flawed humanity, and still love myself, I won't be able to sustain myself in the work of antiracism. There are too many other negative forces at play, let's not lose our sense of humor too!

Through the practice of getting in touch with my inner "superhero power," I cultivate humility, vulnerability, and humor in order to show up better for everyone around me (myself included).

WRITING EXERCISE

1. Your "superhero power": What does your behavior in racial justice spaces suggest about the superpower you wish you had?

2. Your kryptonite: How does your pursuit of that "superhero power" sabotage your participation in the work towards racial justice?

3. Your antidote: What is the small thing you can do, say, or remember when you notice your "superhero power" desires taking over?

MY EXAMPLES

1. Abraham's white anti-racist "superhero power": My behavior in racial justice spaces suggests that I wish I could be liked all the time.

2. My kryptonite: Needing everyone to approve of me all the time leads to overcommitment, burnout, unequal power dynamics, and inevitable disappointment on all sides.

3. My antidote: When I feel fear of not being liked, I say to myself, "When everything else falls away, I will face the mirror." This means that when I die, others' views of me and my life will cease to matter, and I will be held accountable for having lived a life of integrity. It doesn't mean other people's' feelings or thoughts about me don't matter, but it means that I have a deeper responsibility to be true to myself.

Artist: Rebecca Frederick
Poetry: Laura Hershey

CONTEMPLATIVE PRACTICES

How do I let myself be vulnerable to break white silence around racism? I am not sure I have the best words for this, but I will try.

A lot of how I break silence begins in silence. I am a regular attender to my local Quaker meeting and my spiritual practice means that I spend time in silent prayer and meditation. To a large degree this kind of seeking is about sitting with the questions more so than rushing to find the answers. Of course I listen, and I read, and I ask, and I research, and I watch and I learn. But at some point I have to take all that in and actually DO something with it. And that doing actually starts in not doing.

It's hard to sometimes be silent and just be present in the messy swirl of our hurried brains. When I sit in that silence there is a deep tension, a never ending wrestling wherein I try to make sense of injustice; I try to understand why folks choose fear and hate. I wrestle with large order concepts like democracy and economy and who writes history. The silence is a place where I try to figure out how to take action in a way that is effective. I contemplate how a busy mom like myself can balance out making sense of a whole wide world of pain with my tiny, tiny place in it.

It's a place I work through my own fears and worries, some valid, others not so much.

In other words, silence is seldom fully serene or filled with peace—at least not at the onset. It is a place of tension and struggle. The peace sometimes comes. But it takes a while to get there.

Sometimes I come out of the silence with a realization, a plan to move forward, a kind of clarity I didn't have before. Those moments are clear, like a bell. Sometimes I come out of the silence much like I entered in: Confused, scared, angry, a general sense of agitation. Sometimes my bones hurt.

I guess I still sometimes think I'll find an answer in those moments. And sometimes I do! But sometimes there just isn't one. At least not at that moment. Sometimes the answer is just sitting in that tension, knowing that we still have to get up and start building better world for our kids within the confusion. Knowing how much is at stake. Knowing there are so many people who can not turn away.

There will never be a time when everything will make sense. There will never be a strategy written that will tie all the yarns together. When I learn to sit in the tension, I learn to not give up. I learn to accept my own messiness. I learn to get over myself and do real work. So, I guess my point here is that silence reminds me to not be silent. It reminds me to keep building, even as I stumble a billion times. It reminds me that the tension I feel within myself is not to be feared, but rather to be cultivated.

A practice that I use to show up for racial justice shows up in how I prepare for sermons on Sunday and in my ministry.

I drive a lot these days, back and forth between Nashville and the small church where I am humbled to serve as pastor, so I spend a lot of time singing the hymns I learned as a child. Or I sing songs that my partner and I make up and sing to each other. Or I'll call my people—my dear friends/family who need me or whom I need, or my parents, or others.

But mostly I just sit in silence and think about the sermon I'm asked to give on a weekly basis. I listen for where my body/ mind/soul is at while driving past Confederate flags, past a landscape drenched in what is often the invisible blood and memories of people whom my ancestors have attempted to annihilate. And so my ministry, if I'm allowed to have it, is an effort to redeem my ancestors, my people; and my vulnerability in this season of history is the great gift I receive from those who are willing to acknowledge that the redemption of my people is possible.

To that end, the sermon I gave recently was on Luke 10:25-37, where Jesus talks about how the Samaritan saved the man whose ass was whooped by a bunch of thieves. I included an anecdote I heard over the weekend from Anthony Smith, whose powerful ministry in the county seat of my home county, Rowan County, is breaking open the possibility of redemption in ways I'd never experienced there before. Below is a selection from the sermon and my attempt at how to show up as a white person of faith.

"The Black pastor looked at the six white men, and then looked at their guns ... and then he invited each of them to join their bible study ... He asked each man to join a different group, and so each of them joined a different circle of church members, and then together, they read stories about the nonviolence of Jesus.

The bible study lasted for a couple of hours, and each of the six men stayed until the end of the evening. As they came back together to walk out the door, the pastor approached them with a word of peace. And the six men thanked him, told him how much they were grateful for the church's hospitality, and apologized for their original goal, which was to intimidate the pastor with guns on their hips, to provoke him into fear and violence. They shook hands and left, and have never returned."

What we might take from the story of the Black pastor and the six white men with guns is a spin on the story of the Good Samaritan. You see, I think the Good Samaritan is the pastor whom the six men have marginalized; and I think the six white men are lying in a ditch, robbed of their own human dignity and losing their bodies and memories and souls to the poisoned wells of white supremacy. And if the Good Samaritan is the surprising example of the way that a compassionate God can move through those whom we have chosen to marginalize from our community, then the six men are among the consequences of white people's willingness to let that sin continue.

And in the midst of this last week's awful violence, the Samaritan is the 21st century Black freedom struggle, which has once again invited people to proclaim that Black people are human beings, that Black people are children of God. And the man in the ditch is the white society in which most of us grew up, regardless of our generation, a society that taught us to feel disgust at the Black person, a society that taught us to mock Black culture and render black children unworthy of God's love. This is the society that has reduced the humanity of some, and therefore threatens the humanity of us all.

Yes, if we are concerned about the state of the world and the communities in which Black people are dying at alarming rates at the hands of police of officers; if we fear a world in which police officers are shot at the hands of an angry veteran; if we live in fear of the violence that this world is bringing down upon us ... the answer is not to turn our fear into a line in the sand and say "do not cross." The answer is to look up from the ditch at the Samaritan savior who crosses our path and say, "I will let you heal me."

Margaret Anne Ernst, Tennessee

This prayer practice is an adaptation of Ignatius of Loyola's Examen, a discipline of prayerful reflection on one's day.

Here are the questions I've been challenging myself to pray and reflect on before I go to bed in the last couple weeks. They are intended to help calibrate my emotions as I overlook the day especially so as to work against white fragility (which for me crops up particularly in the midnight hour):

1. When did I make a conscious decision today to stand up against racism and for collective liberation?

2. Where was there grief or confusion in my heart today?

3. Where was there joy in my heart today?

4. How could I have been a better accomplice for people in situations of oppression different from my own today?

5. When did someone extend compassion and forgiveness to me today?

6. Where do I need to show compassion and forgiveness for others and for myself going forward into tomorrow?

I explain more in the video about how this practice brings me balance and focus so I can bring my best, growing and learning self to the struggle instead of getting stuck in the "paralysis of (self-)analysis."

Reflective prayer practice:
(https://www.youtube.com/watch?v=sEybPyecZ5I& feature=youtu.be)

Cleve May, North Carolina

Confession as Freedom

White Confession Matters. Yes, I know... all peoples' confession matters. But if we are to reclaim our humanity in a racist arrangement of the world that depends upon our bondage to perverted patterns of being, we must declare, "White Confession Matters."

In the theological tradition that has formed me, we talk about sin as anything that distorts our humanity, destroys human community, and keeps us in bondage to these distorting and destroying patterns. Under this rubric, whiteness, racism and race are sin, plain and simple. These are historical inventions created with the explicit and pernicious purpose of arranging power in ways that establish, perpetuate and preserve a social hierarchy in which folks raced-as-white inhabit and enact violent social, political and economic dominance over everyone else. This arrangement of power is sin; and, ironically, we who are called "white" are the most bound-up folks in this system.

The theological tradition of my church has also formed me to believe that confession is emancipation from bondage to sin. We do not confess our sins so that we will be forgiven; we confess freely because we have been forgiven. We believe in a God who does not wait for us to get our act together before declaring us beloved, but rather who loves us in the midst of our mess so that we can freely come to confession. Only if this is true can confession be a non-coercive act, an act in which we aren't trying to convince God of anything. In confession we are simply receiving the gift of freedom, through which we learn to identify and publicly reject the false identities that have pirated our lives and kept us from our true selves. Confession is a bold declaration that we are more than whiteness has allowed us to be. Confession is a way we begin to move toward liberation, toward a non-distorted humanity, toward our true identities. Confession is freedom on the way to freedom.

For people raced-as-white, confession must include regular naming of the reality that our imaginations and ways of being in the world have been profoundly formed by whiteness, racism, and race. Such naming is not reserved for a moment of prayer in worship on Sundays. I have found it necessary, appropriate, and freeing to practice this mode of confession in everyday conversations, in meetings with administrators at my children's school, in church leadership team meetings, and in community organizing spaces. For example, in a conversation with a friend of color, I once said, "I know that as a white man there are things I have been deeply formed to assume, and things I have been formed not to see. Would you mind helping me think through a question I am wrestling with, so I might recognize some of my racial blinders?" Frequently in meetings with the Equity Team at my kids' school, I will preface comments similarly and explicitly name ways that I have failed to resist my racist formation as a leader and as a father. Such moments of confession have several effects:

1. I experience heightened attentiveness to my racialized defaults and am better able to love the neighbors with whom I am engaging because I am walking in an awareness of the freight my racial identity bears.

2. My confessions contribute to the disarming of defensiveness for other people raced-as-white in the room, and creates a braver space for them to practice confession as a truthful and thus liberating act.

3. Confession increases trust between people of color and myself, and therefore creates greater possibility for racial healing.

Confession is not only resistance to the ways whiteness mal-forms my imagination, it is also a way of reckoning honestly with harm I have created in my complicity with whiteness. I have found it to be a matter of inevitability that I will sometimes act out of my racialized defaults and cause harm to my brothers and sisters of color; I believe this is true for all people raced-as-white.

What is not inevitable, but what alone can mitigate the harm done and keep open the possibility of continued relationship, is the willingness of those of us raced-as-white to practice confession, to own the damage we have done without qualifier, and to ask for forgiveness. Such acts of confession not only honor the brothers or sisters we have harmed, but they serve to deepen our own awareness of the ways whiteness, racism, and race operate upon, in, and through us.

Directly engaging those we hurt with confession, learning from them how our particular transgression participates in and compounds centuries of racist assaults upon their humanity, and experiencing (as I most often have) the power of grace and forgiveness—these things serve as a powerful counter-formation to ways whiteness, racism, and race seek to deform us.

However, confession in these instances must be non-coercive; confession cannot presume a response from those we have harmed. The folks we hurt are not God and they may or may not be able to forgive us for the harm done. So we must remember that confession is first and foremost about our own liberation, about the recovery of our humanity through determined truthfulness and the refusal of fear, paralysis, fragility and defensiveness. We are more than whiteness has told us, so let us confess and be free.

Amber Cullen, Ohio

I wrote this poem after President Trump's inauguration day on January 20th, 2017. The poem stemmed from a deep frustration of white Christian silence and apathy in response to white supremacy. For me, living in close proximity and relationship with communities of color has only served to broaden my understanding of the world, and has been a deep space of healing. Inauguration Day (and all the days before and all the days since) has left me with a prophetic fire in my bones, and a flipping of tables, demanding us as white folk to know and embody a deeper love. Because I know that we can. Because I believe the love of Christ demands the privileged to scoot over at the table, not because it's a 'good deed,' but because it is just.

White Supremacy by Amber Cullen

I come from a long line of cowards
Who know resistance only as a buzzing gnat
By their ear that keeps them from their livelihood
"We cannot flourish with all this noise."

Head tiled in judgement and disgust,
Nose too high to see that beneath their feet are the masses
A space of supremacy only ever to be occupied by
An ever-loving, just God,
And never man.
This is the sin we have never named.

I come from a long line of cowards
Who are too proud to admit that they may have messed up
Too proud to repent
Too proud to embrace

My God
I am sick of your games
And your cowardice makes me ill

If only I might forget that you are
Bones of my bones and flesh of my flesh
But I cannot.

Once I knew the taste of the air by my tilted nose,
Until one day I looked down
And in the masses swam into clarity the face of my brother.
In curiosity I crawled down,
With the firm, supportive grasps of my neighbors,
Only to see that resistance was the lifeblood of the spirit,
Community the medicine of the soul,
And story the tie that binds.
I come from a long line of cowards
Who are so afraid of the unknown of our neighbors
That we will grasp (oh so) tightly to the illusion of
    flourishing
Rather than choosing the courage of repentance,
    mutuality, and healing.
This is the sin we have never named.

More of Amber's writing can be found here:
fb.me/ambercullenculturalorganizer

Beth Howard, Kentucky

A practice that helps me show up when working to create a greater degree of justice in the world comes from my work in recovery.

A slogan in twelve step recovery programs is "Do the next right thing." I've found myself using this as a guiding statement in my life over the past few years. The word "do" is a push to take action. When I'm dealing with fear, especially fear that surfaces around speaking out about injustice, I often spend most of my time thinking and planning, but don't actually do anything. This statement takes the thinking out of the equation and instead pushes me to do something--to put one foot in front of the other, to say something, to show up, to write in solidarity–to do something.

The word "next" helps me remember that I just need to do the next thing, one step at a time. It's a reminder that I do not have to have all the answers or the perfect answer. My action is not going to solve all of the injustices in the world and it doesn't have to. It's just one action I can take right now in the direction of justice.

Another element of this statement that works for me is not just doing any action, but doing what is right. It is my experience that I know what is right in my gut, but I often don't act on it immediately and instead let fear and other negative voices dampen my intuition. Or, I take another action that is less impactful or safer instead of stepping into my vulnerability and doing what I should as a white, anti-racist organizer. This guiding statement reminds me to take right action – that action that my higher self tells me is important and right even if it's scary and I'm unsure.

Perhaps a simple practice like this guiding statement can help us practice showing up. I'm going to try it. I hope you join me.

Virginia Rosenberg, North Carolina

From a place of integration and connection to something greater, I can wisely and sustainably do my part in liberation. It is part spiritual, part practical. It is deeply personal and overwhelmingly collective.

We must recognize common pitfalls of modern spirituality, especially as promoted and practiced in the Western world. Here are some examples, and ways to practically weave together spiritual awareness and activism.

Common pitfalls:

- "Remaining unattached." Choosing to be silent about injustice.

- "Sending Love and Light." Distancing oneself from suffering.

- "Keeping a high vibration." Encouraging numbness and shaming victims of injustice.

- "Emphasizing the spiritual perspective." Negating reality.

- "Privileged preaching." Promoting entitlement and perpetuating privilege.

- "Recreating Tribe." Resisting 'the other' and remaining disassociated from diversity.

How to do better:

- Use your voice. Decide where you stand on issues and make your position clear. Engage in dialogue. Vote. Write representatives. Discuss personal experiences with injustice and talk about current events. Listen to the perspectives others share. Be open to learning more about how oppression operates - both in the world at large and within the individual psyche.

- Cultivate compassion. Prayer is awesome; and it is powerful to pray together. Pray out loud with action. Stand for what you feel is right. Find out what people need and how you can help. Get involved. Explore your role. Identify your unique contributions and employ them.

- Avoid emphasizing the positive. Instead, tell the truth. Encourage emotional expression. Be present with what arises, without attempting to control or change it. Honor anger, sadness, and uncomfortable feelings. Trust them, and embrace feeling them. This develops compassion and strength.

- Respect the lived realities you and others have experienced. Avoid discrediting or discounting lived experience. Witness the real effects of oppression. Put yourself in the shoes of others. Recall a time when you have been a victim and/or an oppressor. Accept mistakes, imperfections, fallibilities, and vulnerabilities of yourself and others. This will help you take ownership over the patterns that promote disparity and motivate change.

- Be humble. Accept that your perspective is limited. Meet people where they are. Avoid making assumptions about others or telling others what to believe. Acknowledge that things happening in the world don't make sense, and we don't need to try to make sense of them. Never blame a victim for their suffering.

- Expand your comfort zone. Build trust and practice healing within communities beyond familiar groups and shared backgrounds of privilege. Create ease and intentional invitations of inclusivity. Explore the social, political, and economic spheres in environments that differ from what is familiar. Learn from willing teachers of varying backgrounds. Create and participate in inclusive spaces to share stories and identify needs. Look for ways to bridge experience, knowledge, and skills to support one another in wholeness.

We can build peace. A true peace. A peace that extends from within and is mirrored in the world outside of us. It takes presence. Compassion. Strength. Dedication. Humility. And it is time. Move beyond the bubble of spiritual separation and enter the world. For as Martin Luther King Jr. said, "no one is free until we are all free." That is a natural truth.

FROM KENTUCKY TO STANDING ROCK: REFLECTIONS FROM TWO WHITE WORKING CLASS WOMEN

By Judi Jennings and Jardana Peacock

Over a year ago, two Kentucky-based white anti-racist activists and writers traveled to Standing Rock. Now, in this time of extreme violence and displacement in our country, we find ourselves returning to our shared but different experiences there. We see the resistance and vision that inspired Standing Rock as a way to inform our forward motion in the world, our social justice work, our spiritual journeys, and our healing.

Jardana Peacock and Judi Jennings both grew up working class and poor. Judi strongly identifies with her Appalachian roots. Jardana, transient most of her life, is now rooted in the South. Judi is an elder in the statewide peace and women's movements. Jardana is a radical healer and spiritual activist. Both answered calls from intergenerational Sioux leaders resisting the Dakota Access Pipeline crossing their sacred lands.

Judi

I traveled with the rising sun from Bismarck, North Dakota, to Camp Oceti Sakowin in early November. The dawn brought with it the realization of how rural landscape is colonized. Unbeckoned images of 1950s western movies flickered through my memories. I recalled this rugged, beautiful landscape being portrayed as a dangerous place, inhabited by violent people.

In Kentucky, British and French colonizers pushed through the Appalachian mountains before the American Revolution, fighting with and against Native tribes. In the 1830s, the US Army forcibly removed the Cherokee from the state. Entire families and whole villages forced to march west in a harsh winter. A few lonely markers still honor the graves of some of those who died along the way. Many—no one knows how many—Cherokee refused to leave and found safety in the Appalachian mountain hollows and caves.

After the Civil War, robber barons, international coal companies and outside lumber businesses exploited the land and natural resources of Appalachia in the name of economic development. Some local white folks joined in the exploitation; some resisted. Yet the landscape was successfully colonized.

So I understand something about loving a land that is appropriated and colonized. I know how claiming a connection to a colonized landscape can be used against you. I have seen how some people will consider you "backwards" and "primitive" for loving that landscape.

Jardana

In the morning, fires lifted with the sun and the call from the elders began at 6am through the loudspeaker. "Come to the ceremony fire," they beckoned us. At the fire, strangers were crammed together. Every time a new person joined, the circle widened to include them. Many of us had never been to an indigenous ceremony before and were uncertain how to act. I have found this uncertainty is a ripe time for the oppression voices to begin to shout within.

In that circle I felt the strong sense that I did not belong. My internalized classism makes me feel like I don't belong unless I have an "official" role to play. This is what a working class identity embeds within you early on in a capitalistic society. Furthermore, the system of white supremacy separates me from other white people and people of color by telling me that I am an individual. Opening my heart into vulnerable connectivity has been a lifelong practice towards reconnection.

Like the smoke licking the edges of fire, a question rose like a ghost, "Who do you come from?" This isn't a question that white people are required to answer very often. Yet, it is one of the most important questions to answer for our personal healing and in healing the divides inside, with earth and with each other. I come from a broken family, as many families are broken. I come from a family with hidden mental and emotional health realities, proud Republican uncles and aunts, working class and poor people, an Italian grandfather who was racist and who deeply desired to make a better life for his family through the promise of an American Dream. A great grandfather who passed down his red hair to my two children from his Danish and Welsh ancestry and drank himself to death under my grandmother's roof. When I piece these parts of a fragmented and painful history together, I viscerally feel the maps of pain that we carry through generation to generation.

Judi

During my time at the camp, participating in the daily flow of outdoor activities and rituals shared by the Sioux, I began to understand my own experience of colonization both as perpetrator and survivor. My loving and hard-working mother took the well worn path of many working class Appalachian whites to assimilate and search for urban opportunities to become middle class. Or maybe she didn't have a choice as a single mom with a child to raise.

When I was a little girl, my mother often took me to visit the rural place where my Great Grandmother lived. She raised my mother, and now I played in her fields and flowers with my cousins. Once, I took a box of mud from the creek back home with me. My Great Grandmother was Cherokee, but we didn't tell people. Because even then, we already knew that many folks would smile and shake their heads like it was some kind of joke. So the ways of my Great Grandmother remained unknown to me. I never learned how she cooked on a wood stove or why she planted her flowers and vegetables in clumps and crooked rows in unexpected places.

I chose not to learn Cherokee ways without even thinking about it. Rather, I excelled in western European learning and ways of thinking. I arrived at Camp Oceti Sakowin with a Ph.D. in British History. But I didn't know how to build a fire or ride horses bareback or how to be Native.

Jardana

An indigenous man visited every person in the fire circle and placed tobacco into hundreds of hands. The elders led us down to the river with the beat of drums and song. "This tobacco is an offering to the river, an offering of our blessings to come now and seven generations from now." As I pressed the tobacco in my palm, I focused on hope, a belief that this violence would end, that the sacred land wouldn't be destroyed by oil, greed and a continuous disconnection from the earth. Our shoes sank into the mud as we held each other from falling, and the brown ribbons of our offerings and blessings floated on the glassy river surface.

Judi

A young Sioux woman told us how she stood armed only with a feather on the banks of the Cannonball River separating the pipeline from the sacred land. An infiltrator pushed her into the river, and the heavily militarized police immediately arrested her and others. After her release, she organized a forgiveness march from a park in a nearby town to the jail. Hundreds of us gathered in a huge circle in the park. She asked us to march in silence with love and forgiveness in our hearts for everyone inside the jail, police and protectors. We marched in silent contemplation. When we reached the jail, she and other local leaders went inside to explain. Then we joined hands in a human chain to encircle the jail. We stood quietly for 30 minutes or more. The silence was more powerful than words.

Jardana

At the women's council, we were asked to organize ourselves, to know who was at camp. We were asked to know our neighbors and take care of the women and children. I was asked by organizers to bring other white people to the decolonization meetings, and to help white people connect to the ways that white supremacy and colonization has hurt us all. I walked from campsite to campsite to meet my neighbors. When I talked with other white folks, I listened and held space for their uncertainties, their feelings of "not doing enough" or "knowing enough" and for making mistakes. I carry these doubts too, I shared. This disconnection from ourselves and each other is how supremacy systems and colonization maintain. At camp, we were asked to reconnect. For so many of us, care, love, ceremony, prayer and story sharing were very new.

Judi

Day by day, the warmth and connectivity around the sacred circle and the evening drumming sessions reminded us of our interconnections. I saw that my individualism meant trusting reason and logic more than prayer and ritual. I became more aware of my connection with the land and people around me through the power of living collectively and practicing forgiveness.

Jardana

At Standing Rock, the times I felt most like myself were when I sat by the river and prayed, meditated and let the oppression of competition, scarcity, superiority and separation fall away. When I met my neighbors and let go of my walls and fears of not belonging, I was held in a community of care and connection.

Jardana and Judi

History matters, it repeats, and the pain of our oppression is passed down through the generations when it goes unhealed. Indigenous activist Winona LaDuke reminds: "We are a part of everything that is beneath us, above us, and around us. Our past is our present, our present is our future, and our future is seven generations past and present."

Colonialism demands that we exploit the environment and extract resources from people without even stopping to think about it. Standing Rock taught us that colonization is complicated. It isn't just something that happened in the past but something that we must continually commit to dismantling inside and out. In whiteness we can too often be blind to the ways that we are interconnected.

"Let earth renew
broken spirits
find precious
love once shared
that will not be forgotten."

bell hooks, *Appalachian Elegy Number 51*

At Standing Rock, we began to examine the often invisible way that settler colonialism plays out in our lives. By participating in ritual, prayer, and ceremony, we felt reconnected to ourselves, each other, and the earth. This is healing. To heal, is to reconnect to what has been lost in colonization and white supremacy—not to erase it but rather to face the ways it shows up inside of our bodies, psyches, spirits, our interpersonal relationships, in our work and in our world. We believe that a return to interconnection for white people requires a deep commitment to dismantling colonialism and oppression.

BUILDING THE WORLD WE NEED: A SYLLABUS

In my spiritual activism, I've learned that history must be the foundation, and spirituality the heart, process and frame of how we build the world we need.

I've learned how to show up as a white antiracist woman, how to work across generation, the important role of love, healing and spirituality in our movement building, and the effects of trauma on our bodies, spirits and movements.

I've learned that systems of oppression are deeply interwoven into our bodies, psyches, and even inside of our social and environmental change organizations.

The work of changemaking is slow and deep, layered and complicated and we haven't yet figured out a formula that doesn't marginalize someone.

I've learned that perfection is a barrier to my own activism and in my connection with others. I've learned that when I make mistakes, when I fall—this is a time for growth and deepening.

I have also come to understand that my journey has in many ways been in preparation for this moment of crisis.

Here are some patterns I see in our changemaking and suggested readings to support a deeper dive.

- **We are at a shifting point.** Regardless of who you are, there is a shift in the energy, the ways we interact, the ways we are more afraid or bolder in our truth and the truth. Priorities have shifted and focus has deepened. The magnifying glass is strong and to look in, is to see the festering wounds that have gone unhealed. White supremacy, colonization, xenophobia, ableism, and queer and transphobia have poisoned the foundations that this country was founded on and it often proliferates in our changemaking.

In the aftermath of the 2017 election, I was unprepared for the division among people on the same side. The critique, the call out culture and the rejection of people based on how radical or not their politics, leadership and Facebook statuses are, is evidence of the healing that must take place within our movements if change is to truly happen.

Divide and conquer is as old as the beginning of humanity. When we divide, we allow ourselves to be fragmented and less powerful. White supremacy wins when we turn on each other.

The wounds of this nation are many, the ground is soaked in the blood of indigenous people, structures were built on the sweat and backs of enslaved Africans, and the white colonizers and those who stood by without resisting this inhumanity, who enacted this genocide and rape—they too have passed down the trauma of being the oppressor.

The wounds are deep. If there was ever a time to heal, to come together, to do the slow and deep work of suturing the divisions—now is the time. To do this will require white folks to do our work of decolonizing, anti-oppression and healing from the chains around our hearts and spirits as we dig deeper into our own ancestry and reconnect to who we are, where we come from and what we have a choice to step into if we do the continual work of liberation.

For all of us, it's a time of examining how we are spending our energy, how we are building and how we are taking care of ourselves and our communities. In order to truly build a beloved community, we all are needed.

For a deeper dive, read:

Our Cynicism Will Not Build a Movement. Collaboration Will by Alicia Garza.

Emergent Strategy by adrienne maree brown.

Remember This When You Talk About Standing Rock by Kelly Hayes.

- **Healers and artists are imperative.** Healing and art is the vision, the sustenance, and the hope of what the future can be. In healing we restore, regenerate and reconnect. In art, we actualize and connect to beauty, imagination and inspiration. Through both, we are held in a process of facing the deep pain of oppression and the hope of liberation. This is the nourishment that will help us survive. It can no longer be treated as marginal.

  Artists and healers have always been at the forefront of revolutions and radical transformation. They have also historically been persecuted and banned.

From native people's persecution because of their spiritual connection to the earth, to the burning of the witches of the 15th and 16th centuries in Europe and the US.

Yet, art heals, and healers support movements, from the cultural organizing foundations of the US and Global South to the growing spiritual activism and healing justice efforts across the world.

Art magnifies our voices, weaves and connects us to the imagination of what is possible. Healers hold essential support and care space. Root workers, midwives, storytellers, cultural organizers, poets, song leaders, magic makers, spiritual leaders and body workers cultivate connection and healing with our ancestors, nourish us in times of pain and equip us with the tools to show up over and over again. Our resilience is strengthened through art and healing.

We need healers and artists more than ever. Contribute to their livelihood so they can create, vision and help us heal. Take the time to connect with nature, art, and your own healing—we need more wholeness.

For a deeper dive, read:

A Not-So-Brief Personal History of Healing Justice Movement, 2010-2016 by Leah Lakshmi Piepzna-Samarasinha.

The Radical Work of Healing: Fania and Angela Davis on a New Kind of Civil Rights Activism by Sarah van Gelder.

- **Rest and resistance.** The needs of our world are immense. However, we are only 100% of a person. We have responsibilities, perhaps kids, community and family and then add on basic survival needs like eating and sleeping.

  Taking on everything is too much and will make us ineffective. Please, consider the trauma, the fear, the pain weighing in the air we breathe and in our bodies and take care. We cannot show up to everything, and definitely not well. We need to show up from a place that is grounded in love and sustainable. When we take care of ourselves and each other, we resist systems of oppression that would have us be martyrs, that would have us be expendable. How we take care is vital to centering liberation in our changemaking. When we rest and restore, we are able to show up and resist, to build the world we need.

  For a deeper dive, read:

  The Urgency of Slowing Down by Kazu Haga.

  I Vow Not to Burn Out by Mushim Patricia Ikeda.

  Be the Change: Six Disabled Activists On Why the Resistance Must Be Accessible.

- **Inside a spiritual moment.** I do not believe that he who does not deserve to be named is a godsend. I do not believe that he is the reason for revolution. History tells us the story of our arrival. Racism is deeply embedded into our culture, psyches, bodies and spirits. We must know our history and know ourselves. This is painful work and it is what will prepare us to show up with humility, clarity and greater dedication. This is spiritual work, inside of a spiritual moment.

For a deeper dive, read:

Something Much Greater At Stake by Michelle Alexander.

The Link Between Soil, Soul and Society By Satish Kumar.

In closing: we are fierce. Healing is needed. Protest is needed. Writing is needed. Art is needed. New organizing efforts are needed. Explore how you fit into one of the many needs. When we show up rooted in histories of resistance, with an openness to change, committed to healing inside and out, and with a will to build, to imagine—we are contributing to the universal arc towards justice. Breathe, and again. It's a long road and as travelers, we must be responsible: drink water, eat food, take care, share resources, let's hold each other up and rest in order to resist for the long haul.

Resources

We are at a shifting point.

- Garza, Alicia. "Our Cynicism Will Not Build a Movement. Collaboration Will." *Mic*, 26 Jan. 2007, https://mic.com/articles/166720/blm-co-founder-protesting-isnt-about-who-can-be-the-most-radical-its-about-winning#.FakbMKZVz.

- brown, adrienne maree. *Emergent Strategy*. AK Press. 2017.

- Hayes, Kelly. "Remember This When You Talk About Standing Rock." *Yes! Magazine*, 29 Oct. 2016, http://www.yesmagazine.org/how-to-talk-about-standing-rock-20161028.

Healers and artists are imperative

- Piepzna-Samarasinha, Leah Lakshmi. "A Not-So-Brief Personal History of Healing Justice Movement, 2010-2016." *Mice Magazine*, Fall 2016, http://micemagazine.ca/issue-two/not-so-brief-personal-history-healing-justice-movement-2010-2016.

- van Gelder, Sarah. "The Radical Work of Fania and Angela Davis On A New Kind of Civil Rights Activism." *Yes! Magazine*, 18 Feb. 2006, http://www.yesmagazine.org/issues/life-after-oil/the-radical-work-of-healing-fania-and-angela-davis-on-a-new-kind-of-civil-rights-activism-20160218.

Rest and resistance

- Haga, Kazu. "The Urgency of Slowing Down." *Waging Non-Violence*, 25 January 2017, https://wagingnonviolence.org/feature/urgency-slowing-down.

- Ikeda, Mushim Patricia. "I Vow Not to Burn Out." *Lions Roar*, 26 March 2018, https://www.lionsroar.com/i-vow-not-to-burn-out.

- "Be the Change: Six Disabled Activists On Why the Resistance Must Be Accessible." *Auto Straddle*, 13 Feb. 2017, https://www.autostraddle.com/be-the-change-six-disabled-activists-on-why-the-resistance-must-be-accessible-368956.

Inside a spiritual moment

- Alexander, Michelle. "Something Much Greater At Stake." *Radical Discipleship*, 18 Sept. 2016, https://radicaldiscipleship.net/2016/09/18/something-much-greater-at-stake.

- Kumar, Satish. "The Link Between Soil, Soul and Society." *The Guardian*, 16 Sept. 2016, https://www.theguardian.com/sustainable-business/satish-kumar-soil-soul-society.

A WAY FORWARD

We have a unique opportunity in this moment in time to alter the course of history. Our increased understanding of neuroscience and the mind and body connection can inform how we move forward, if we tap into those lessons. Gloria E. Anzaldúa, a Latinx lesbian feminist writer and scholar wrote, "I change myself, I change the world." As we better integrate the connections between the mind and the body, it's evident that we must explore our own pain in the processes of working to change the pain of the world. In fact, that is part of ending injustice.

The violence of injustice is painful and we must also find ways to take action to end that violence. Whether that is through writing, participating in demonstrations, creating art for social change, education, organizing or healing—so many actions are needed to eradicate these injustices. Social change happens inside and outside and wellness and spirituality are both vital to ground and inform that internal and external process.

We can change the world together.

In the protests and organizing work of Black Lives Matter, and at Standing Rock, healers have been front and center. The language and conversation has been focused around generational trauma from white supremacy, racism and oppression and the need to heal from it. Although activists are still burning out and becoming overwhelmed, this is a start towards making the conversation more central in our movements and organizing work. Wellness and spirituality can no longer be at the margins.

People of Color and Indigenous leaders have long held the importance of healing, love and spirituality as foundational for movements of social change. There is a long tradition at the Allied Media Conference of healing justice practitioners offering holistic healing services and analysis to that conference and in their communities at home. There is much to learn from groups and organizations such as Betty's Daughter Arts Collaborative, Black Lives Matter, Sage Community Health Collective, Harriet's Apothecary, Octavia's Brood, Soul Force, Southerners on New Ground (SONG), Third Root Community Health Center, Spirit House, Movement Generation, Movement Strategy Center, Rockwood Leadership Institute and the best practices of organizations that are no longer operating such as Stone Circles at the Stone House and Kindred Southern Healing Justice Collective.

Social movements are vital for us to create the larger systemic changes we need so that we can have healthy communities; institutions, families, and lives based in liberation, feminist, and anti-racist values. That's why it's so important that change makers are engaged in a journey of healing, so that we can both be present in our lives and also more effective in bringing about visionary change. In order for our social justice movements to be well, activists, organizers, educators, artists and leaders must also be well. This is a different kind of leadership.

Showing up to practice on an almost daily basis takes effort and dedication that is only possible with trial and failure, with fear and light and with isolation and support. When we go into the pain we find the most brilliant light. This is the power of practice.

Below I provide seven offerings for bringing practice into your work, communities and organizations. I created this document for a workshop I created with Ebony Noelle Golden of Betty's Daughter Arts Collaborative for the Highlander Research and Education Center's Zilphia Horton Cultural Organizing Institute directed by Tufara Waller Muhammad.

7 OFFERINGS FOR CREATING HEALING AND SPIRITUAL SPACE[5]

▽ Create ritual every day. Open with a symbolic gesture. Light a candle, ring a bell, share a poem. Mark a space sacred. This calls people into shared space together: it is sacred space, space we cherish that cherishes those who help create it.

▽ Gratitude circle. At the end of the day come into a circle. One person begins and turns to their right or left and gives gratitude for something the person next to them did that day. It can be something the person shared, a way that they reached out to another person in kindness, and a way they contributed to the space. It should be specific. This is about deep listening and witnessing. A way to see each other.

▽ Give appreciation. At the beginning of your time together everyone picks a name of someone else in the group. Everyone holds this person in their hearts and sends good and encouraging energy to this person. At the end of a specific time period, each person writes a letter (creates something) of gratitude and hope for the person and their journey ahead and shares it with them.

---

5 Compiled from the principles and practices of the Kentucky Remembers! Youth Human Rights Project, Yoga, Rockwood Leadership Institute, Women Building Power in Kentucky, Stone Circles at the Stone House, The Highlander Center, The Kentucky Foundation for Women's Special Project, Friends, Family and Community.

▽ Create an optional space for meditation and yoga in the morning/night. This can be seated or walking meditation. Walking meditation is about being intentional of every step you take. Focusing on one-pointedness, one step after another. Breathe and let the mind relax. When we quiet the chatter inside we gain space to think with more clarity. Meditative practices are great any time but are also restorative ways to open or close a day or a space. Yoga Nidra is a deep relaxation practice that doesn't require much movement at all and is restorative and healing. Yoga Nidra and other meditative practices help with sleep. Yoga and meditation is about release and breath so that more space can be created internally.

▽ Land is spiritual. Each season, breeze, landscape is an invitation to appreciate the natural world around you. Creating art through an interaction with the land is a meditative practice. Find objects on land. What are the ways they inspire you? Listen to the sounds of the natural world and create a dance, a monologue of the voices of people who have helped create the space you occupy, or create a visual compilation of found objects.

▽ Create meditative space where you are; identify touchstones that can remind you of meditative practice and breath. There is a beautiful book by Thich Nhat Hanh called *Creating Space, Creating a Home Meditation Practice*. This is a small but powerful book that can guide you.

▽ Build space together. Art making and organizing encourage us to create space together. How can we also integrate wellness, spiritual practice and transformation into these spaces? What are symbolic representations of the spaces we want to create where wellness and transformation is possible? Integrate these into the space. Create a labyrinth, paint a canvas together, or build something beautiful.

SHOWING UP FOR LIBERATION

Practice begins with one. Above you will find many offerings from white antiracist leaders across the US. Try these, one at a time, in a study group, in your political work, and/or your practice or faith community. When we center healing and spirituality, our ability to show up for racial justice shifts, and we contribute towards building a stronger movement for justice inside and out.

JOURNAL QUESTIONS

1. *What does practice mean to me?*

2. *How is my current practice (defined as ways I connect with my inner wisdom, truth, love, earth and/or Spirit) connected to my practice in the world?*

3. *How does practice show up in my place of work, in my culture, in my community?*

4. *What are the narratives playing inside my head? Are these helpful or harmful? How so?*

5. *How can I integrate practice more into my life and work? What is one promise I can make to myself?*

How White Folks Can Show Up For Racial Justice

I remember the first day of my Civil Rights class at Northern Kentucky University.

An older white woman with a white bob cut, large owl glasses and a soft presence greeted us. Her name was Anne Braden. I was prepared to crack open my book and start digging into the archives of history.

Anne asked us to push our books aside and take out a piece of paper instead. "Write down the first time you realized there is racism." I sat with my pen perched in pause. I kept trying to dig deeper and deeper into my life. There had to be an earlier time when I became aware of racism. However, there wasn't. I hadn't fully understood that racism existed until the age of seventeen. The realization shocked me.

Anne never did ask us to open that book. A long-time journalist and Southern organizer, Anne taught us that history is always happening and that we must choose which side of it to step into. Anne told stories about racial justice organizing in Louisville, Kentucky and all across the south. She shared personal stories about Martin Luther King, Jr. and people I'd never heard of, like Fannie Lou Hamer and Ella Baker. She lifted up student activism on campus and always made room to discuss current events and campus activism.

I soon joined the campus activist group, Students Together Against Racism (STAR). There I learned how to listen to people of color, the importance of building relationships with other white folks in order to hold each other accountable in our privilege, and how important it is for white folks to study and learn the real history of the United States, told by those most affected. Anne gave me a language for understanding what I could be: an antiracist white person.

One day, I shared with Anne that I planned to study sociology and focus on criminology in graduate school. She cocked her head and raised her eyebrows, and then she asked, "Why?" I talked with her about a youth center I had worked at and how the kids there were being criminalized because of their race.

"What are you going to do with a degree like that, though? What are you going to do?"

I paused and thought about it, and then I got it. She was asking me how I was planning to use my white body to interrupt racism. Anne advocated for students to embody justice and constantly question our motives. Were they based in dismantling white supremacy or upholding our own privileges?

I altered my path and moved to Louisville, Kentucky, where I joined a powerful community of white, Black and Latinx people, many of whom, like me, were Anne's mentees.

That was over a decade ago, yet the racism and state violence against Black and Brown bodies continues. Since the death of Trayvon Martin, I have seen an awakening occur for many white people, especially young folks and people of faith.

Lately, I've been reflecting on my journey as a white antiracist in an effort to understand how to better show up for racial justice and bring others along for the journey. Here are a few of the key cornerstones I've identified.

1. Mentorship.

Mentorship is a mirror that reflects back to us our divinity. So many young activists I've talked with and coached struggle with finding a mentor. Let's expand our definitions of mentorship. Mentorship can look like calling on our ancestors or heroines to guide us. Mentorship may be the connection we feel in the natural world, it can come from a peer or even a child. Our yoga, meditation and prayer practices can act as a mentor for us, mirroring back to us where we struggle, where we can go deeper and how vital we are to this world. We need this mirror to ground us and support us to show up, especially when it's hard. As white folks, as younger and older changemakers, we will make mistakes. Our mentors hold us and love us exactly as we are, helping us to show up to our imperfections with courage.

2. Be emotional.

In the Western world there is an often-unspoken belief that to be emotional is to be weak. However, injustice is an affront to our hearts and our spirits, which desire and need connection. When we feel the pain and trauma of the world, we connect to the humanity of others. To feel allows us to go deeper than the intellectual exercise of browsing a Facebook post or skimming a news story. When we feel the weight of the loss of Black and Brown lives in the world, we interrupt racism's intention to divide and separate us from each other. When we feel, we move beyond the intellectual and into the body. Present in our body, we then can begin to integrate, heal and embody our values in the world.

3. Show up.

We don't have to yell into a megaphone, attend protests or even get arrested to be an activist. Showing up looks like people across race linking arms on the picket line, but it also looks like hard conversations with friends and family. Showing up looks like joining a Showing up for Racial Justice (SURJ) chapter meeting even when we don't know anyone in the group. Showing up looks like writing a post on Facebook, sharing a blog post and placing our bodies in public for racial justice. Showing up helps us determine how we can embody our values in the world. We create change when we show up.

When we show up in our fully broken states, then we heal, then we build, then we deepen our capacity to love each other and ourselves.

I know it's uncomfortable, my people, but this is our history. What will our legacy be? Will it be one of white silence, or imperfect but embodied action toward racial justice? I have been working with other white folks to create practices to help us to step into our more courageous leadership.

We can do this.

ABOUT THE CREATOR AND AUTHOR

Jardana Peacock is a writer, a spiritual activist and a healer. She is the founder of Liberation School and Liberatory Leadership Project, which works to center spirituality and healing into movements for change.

She has been studying and practicing subtle energetics, body-based healing, spiritual healing and traditional yoga for over 17 years and is a 500 hour certified yoga teacher.

A longtime movement builder and organizer, she's worked on racial justice, LGBTQ rights and economic justice, helping to found the U.S. based network, Showing Up for Racial Justice (SURJ), training a global field of changemakers through her cultural organizing work at the Highlander Research and Education Center and currently in supporting organizers and social justice leaders in New York, London, Mexico City and other urban and rural centers.

She lives in Louisville, Kentucky. Reach her at www.jardanapeacock.com. Schedule a book reading or workshop, jardana@jardanapeacock.com.

EDITOR AND COMMUNITY OUTREACH

Susannah Bartlow is a writer, educator, organizer and yoga practitioner who first learned spirituality and social justice growing up in a feminist Methodist family in Philadelphia. Those seeds grew into a high-intensity, higher education career focusing on feminist racial justice and anti-violence work; after a dramatic exit, she began a second middle life as a case manager/trauma specialist with youth in Milwaukee. She currently lives in Memphis, Tennessee teaching and working in Memphis schools and communities on the path to a career as a therapist for movement/social change workers. You can find out more about her work at www.susannahbartlow.com.

ABOUT THE CONTRIBUTORS

William Brummett is a faculty at Liberation School, a healing and spiritual school for changemakers. He is a current member and two-time Steering Committee member of Stay Together Appalachian Youth (STAY), a youth-led project in Appalachia that works to develop economic opportunities for young people to stay and thrive in the region. He is a former Niswonger Scholar committed to building the leadership of Appalachian young people in the northeast Tennessee region. Additionally, he's worked at the Highlander Research and Education Center and Stone Circles at the Stone House, an activist retreat center formerly located in Mebane, NC and founded by Claudia Horwitz. He is an artist, an activist and a lover of nature. He is a graduate of Elon University where he majored in Religious Studies and minored in Political Science and Nonviolence Studies.

Kate Cavanagh is a mother who is part of a big extended Italian and Irish-American family, grew up in Northwest New Jersey, and is a school social worker. She lives in Brooklyn, NY, where she is an anti-racist activist and facilitates community self healing circles through Urban Atabex. She has a vision of a world where people are connected authentically to the earth and each other through ritual, practice and community.

Mike Clawson is the founder of The Spiritual Transformation Project, a new network of religious communities, spiritual practitioners, activists, artists, and non-profits working at the intersection of spirituality and social change. An activist, author, and scholar, Clawson holds a PhD in Religion from Baylor University, with a focus on the ways religion is evolving in the twenty-first century. He has been a youth pastor, church planter, and National Cohorts Coordinator for Emergent Village. He currently lives in Austin with his two children and regularly teaches as an adjunct faculty member at both Austin Presbyterian Theological Seminary and the Episcopal Seminary of the Southwest.

Willa Conway comes from a lineage of fierce women – white settler colonial capitalists, writers, artists, addicts, mystics, truth tellers, humans who have harmed and been harmed. She works with Shakti Rising, Solidaire Network, Resource Generation, and generative somatics to look at and feel into the ways that wealth, gender, and trauma intersect across the economic spectrum. In 2017, Willa founded the Weavers Fellowship, which funds Black organizers and artists predominantly in the U.S. South. Willa believes that the revolution is alive and well and that in the movement we have all that we need to continue to take bold steps to heal ourselves, our communities, and change the philanthropic and economic landscape of this country. Willa accesses her power through daily walks with coffee, music, and sunshine. You can reach her at willa. conway@gmail.com.

Amber Cullen is a cultural organizer based in Akron, Ohio, who is learning to lead a life of active repentance from White supremacy towards the work of collective healing and flourishing. She is currently the Director of Communications and Advocacy at South Street Ministries (a member of the Christian Community Development Association), and the Artistic Director of VIBE Collective—a hub of artists in the intersection of art, culture, and education who seek to create spaces for community transformation and healing. Originally from Akron, Amber's story has taken her from her hometown, to the corn fields, to row homes, to the shores, and back to Akron once again, with a deep conviction that we can care for one another better. She is currently writing a memoir, and her visual art, which explores paradox and place through Midwestern eyes, can be found on Etsy at *theologyinparadox*.

Margaret Anne Ernst is the proud daughter of Cindy and Carla and is a queer, faith-rooted, organizer and movement chaplain currently living in Nashville, TN. For the past 8 years, Margaret has been in service to various economic, racial and immigration justice struggles in the Philadelphia area and in mid-Tennessee. She holds a special commitment to inviting white people into anti-racist action and is in the process of seeking ordination in the United Church of Christ. Her primary spiritual practices are singing and laughing, "especially when it is not necessarily prescribed," (Mary Oliver).

Rebecca Frederick is a working class artist, organizer, and badass single mom. She lives and creates with her 3 children and dying house plants in Louisville, Ky. Rebecca believes strongly in the need for our movements to be built in multigenerational ways, allowing space for every generation in leadership and action. Using art and cultural organizing Rebecca organizes working families into action, community and power building with an anti-racist focus, lifting up the voices and stories of Black and Brown folks.

Laura Hershey (1962 – 2010) was a Colorado poet, writer, activist. Her poems have appeared in Calyx, Shakespeare's Monkey Review, Trillium Literary Journal, wordgathering.com, the anthology Fire in the Soul: 100 Poems for Human Rights, and her book "Spark after Dark." She has written essays for Ms., off our backs, Waccamaw Journal, National Parks, and U.S. News & World Report, and many other publications.

Beth Howard is an organizer working with the Central Kentucky Chapter of KFTC. Beth grew up in West Liberty (Morgan County). She is a graduate of Eastern Kentucky University with a Master's in English with an emphasis in Creative Writing. Beth served for five years as a lead organizer with a grassroots organization in Daytona Beach, Florida called Fighting Against Injustice Toward Harmony (FAITH). She returned to Kentucky in 2011 and worked as a case manager facilitating classes in parenting, job coaching, and interpersonal skills for a multi-county program based in West Liberty. Beth is currently completing her 300 hour Yoga Teacher training under the guidance of Vira Bhava Yoga in Boone, North Carolina.

Carol J. Kraemer is a community activist and cultural worker who has worked for civil rights in her native, Louisville, KY for 30 years. In 1988 she co-founded the lesbian rock band, Yer Girlfriend, and continues to write and play music in support of progressive causes. She has worked as a volunteer and on staff of the Fairness Campaign, the LGBTQ rights group in Louisville, KY since 1991 and has been active in struggles for a workers' rights, immigrant rights and against police abuse. After traveling to Cuba with the Henry Wallace Brigade in 2006 she became involved with efforts to free the Cuban Five.

She currently serves on the board of the Carl Braden Memorial Center and is a co-founder and leadership team member of Louisville Showing Up for Racial Justice (LSURJ). Carol is the Director of the Davis-Putter Scholarship Fund which provides grants for student activists working for radical change.

Jes Kelley is one in a long line of subversive southerners. She has had the honor of leading various social justice trainings for nearly 15 years. Her life has been shaped by the legacy of people fighting for queer liberation, reproductive justice and anti-racism. She believes in possibility, in the importance of bringing a trauma-informed lens to anti-oppression work, and that no one is disposable.

Maggie MacLeod is a social worker, healer, and yoga therapist based in Durham, NC. She is committed to addressing both interpersonal and systemic trauma. Maggie specializes in healing from sexual trauma and the effects of mass incarceration through a unique combination of movement, touch, meditation and talk therapy. She enjoys spending time with her husband, healing justice enthusiasts, animals, and taking deep dives into quirky TV shows.

Meredith Martin-Moats is an anti-racist organizer based in Little Rock, Arkansas. She founded the McElroy House, a center for rural folks of Arkansas to interact with culture and political education. She is a public historian and produces radio pieces for KUAF 91.3 FM, Public Radio out of Fayetteville, Arkansas and writes for the The Courier, a local newspaper out of Russellville, Arkansas, among others. She works as an editor and transcriber for the Pryor Center for Arkansas Oral and Visual History at the University of Arkansas. Additionally, she organizes a caregiver group in Arkansas and is an active member at her Quaker church community.

Rev. Allyn Maxfield-Steele Raised in Texas, Germany and North Carolina, Rev. Allyn Maxfield-Steele's movement work has included solidarity struggles with Thai people's movements, work as an educator and organizer in Spartanburg, South Carolina, and a range of support for front-line struggles in Nashville, Tennessee, and throughout the South and Appalachia. An ordained minister in the Christian Church (Disciples of Christ), Allyn has served congregations in Juneau, Alaska, Nashville, and Springfield, TN. Allyn holds a B.A. in History from Wofford College (SC) and a Masters of Divinity from Vanderbilt Divinity School. He is co-director at the Highlander Research and Education Center, located in east Tennessee.

Cleve May is a husband and father of four in Durham, NC, where he helps lead a United Methodist church that is learning to engage Christian practices in ways that liberate folks from whiteness.

Harley Meyer is a Chicago trans/plant to rural Vermont. Harley continues to be inspired by deep time spent in Oventic, Chiapas, the Highlander Center, and with their Democratic Education Collective comrades at Sarah Lawrence College. They have a degree in Human Geography and are looking forward to further education in poetry, seed saving/sovereignty, and food justice. They work at Sterling College and aspire to farm, write, and build rural movement community in Central Vermont. Harley is the author of Emergency Healing, published by Deadly Chaps Press with work nominated for the 2011 Pushcart Prize.

kate poole (artist) is an inheritor of wealth and a financial activist working to move resources to the solidarity economy. she is an integrated capital fellow at rsf social finance, co-founder of be invested (beinvestedtogether.com) and is building a wealth management firm focused on reparations and wealth redistribution. she loves feminist performance art, authentic movement, and her partner, who is also named kate. you can read her comics at comicsbykate.com or reach out to her at beinvestedwithkate@gmail.com.

Virginia Rosenberg is an Intuitive Astrologer and Movement Artist; movement in the body and progressive social movement. Virginia's main interest is natural healing of self and society, and she views astrology and movement as effective tools for liberation. Virginia has offered thousands of readings and leads retreats, classes, and workshops. Her educational background includes post-colonial and women's/gender studies, anthropology, journalism, documentary filmmaking, Eastern philosophy, dance, Taoist internal martial arts, spiritual alchemy, ritual and ceremony, and energy work. Learn more about her writing and work here: www.VirginiaRosenberg.com

Rev. Dr. Michelle Walsh, LICSW is a Lecturer at the Boston University School of Social Work and the author of Violent Trauma, Culture, and Power: An Interdisciplinary Exploration in Lived Religion. She and her husband, Rev. Clyde Grubbs, both Unitarian Universalist clergy, also share a community ministry providing spiritual direction, coaching, workshops, and consulting for activists and those seeking to become more active in anti-oppression work. More information can be found at www.revmichellewalsh.com.

RESOURCE LIST

This resource list was crowd sourced and is by no means comprehensive.

Trainings and Community

C-Integral, www.c-integral.org.

The Icarus Project, www.theicarusproject.net/hireus.

Liberatory Leadership Project and Liberation School, www.liberatoryleadership.org.

The People's Institute for Survival and Beyond, www.pisab.org.

Racial Equity Institute, www.racialequityinstitute.org.

Showing Up for Racial Justice, www.surj.org.

your local SURJ chapter.

Training for Change, www.trainingforchange.org.

Healing-Based Organizations

adrienne maree brown and Emergent Strategy, www.adriennemareebrown.net.

Alice's Garden, www.alicesgardenmke.com.

Allied Media Conference, www.alliedmedia.org.

Alternate Roots, www.alternateroots.org.

Anacostia Yogi, www.anacostiayogi.com.

Betty's Daughter Arts Collaborative, www.bettysdaughterarts.com.

Black Lives Matter, www.blacklivesmatter.com.

Center for Transformative Change, www.transformativechange.org.

CentroAshe, www.centroashe.org.

Core/el Centro, www.core-elcentro.org.

CTZNWELL, www.ctznwell.org.

Datule' Artist Collective, www.facebook.com/DatuleArtistCollective/?timeline_context_item_type=intro_card_work&timeline_context_item_source=566002587.

DC Wellness Tree, www.dcwellnesstree.ning.com.

Escuela Ki'kotemal, www.escuelakikotemal.wordpress.com.

Faith Matters Network, www.faithmattersnetwork.org.

Four Corners Wellness, www.4cornersyogawellness.com.

Freed Bodyworks, www.freedbodyworks.com.

Freedom Beyond.

Generative Somatics, www.generativesomatics.org.

Harriet's Apothecary, www.harrietsapothecary.com.

Healing Hub Community, www.healinghub.community.

Healing Justice Podcast, www.healingjustice.org.

Highlander Research and Education Center, www.highlandercenter.org.

The Institute for Somatics and Social Justice,
    www.somaticsandsocialjustice.org.

The Juice Kitchen, www.thejuicekitchenmke.com.

Movement Strategy Center, www.movementstrategy.org.

The Mystic Soul Project, www.mysticsoulproject.com.

National Queer and Transgender Therapists of Color Network,
    www.nqttcn.com.

OmTownYogis, www.omtownyogis.org.

People's Movement Center, www.peoplesmovementcenter.com.

Rhythm Science Sound, www.rhythmsciencesound.com.

Rockwood Leadership Institute, www.rockwoodleadership.org.

Sage Community Health, www.sagecommunityhealth.org (no
    longer active).

Sister Circle Collective, www.sistercirclecollective.org.

SONG, www.southernersonnewground.org.

Soul Force, www.soulforce.org.

Spirit House, www.spirithouse-nc.org.

Third Root Community Health Center, www.thirdroot.org.

This Bridge Called Our Health,
    www.thisbridgecalledourhealth.wordpress.com.

Universal Partnership, www.universalpartnership.org.

The Well DC, www.bewelldc.com.

The Zen Dragonfly, www.thezendragonfly.com.

Antiracist Practitioners (by last name)

Healing in Our Times Project, www.jadetperry.com/healing-in-%20 our-times-project.

Patty Adams, www.instagram.com/liberate2heal.

Bayo Akomolafe, www.bayoakomolafe.net.

Jacoby Ballard, www.jacobyballard.com.

Susannah Bartlow, www.susannahbartlow.com.

Anna Bethea, www.uua.org/offices/people/anna-bethea.

Dr. Michele Berger, www./womensstudies.unc.edu/people/faculty/ michele-tracy-berger.

devynn emory, www.sage-massage.com.

Richael Faithful, www.richaelfaithful.com.

Kelly Germaine, www.kellygermaine.com.

Lauren Giambrone, www.goodfightherbco.com.

Beth Godbee, www.heart-head-hands.com.

Heather Hackman, www.hackmanconsultinggroup.org.

Bear Hebert, www.bearteachesyoga.org.

Tada Hozumi, www.selfishactivist.com/work-with-me.

Chanelle John, www.facebook.com/hivesoulyoga.

Micky ScottBey Jones, www.mickyscottbeyjones.com.

Andréa Ranae Johnson, www.andrearanae.com.

Molly Kitchen, www.mollykitchen.com.

Eric Law, www.kscopeinstitute.org.

Pam Lozoff, www.spiritofyouthyoga.com/pam-lozoff.

Teresa Pasquale Mateus, www.teresapasqualemateus.com.

Maggie (Cohen) MacLeod, www.maggiecohenyoga.com.

Dori Midnight, www.dorilandia.com.

Maryse Mitchell-Brody, www.reachmaryse.com.

Rusia Mohiuddin, www.universalpartnership.org/rusia.

Mari Mujica, www.marimujica.com.

Jennifer Patterson & Corpus Ritual, www.fthebody.net.

Jardana Peacock, www.jardanapeacock.com.

Virginia Rosenberg, www.virginiarosenberg.com.

Sheena Sood, www.leeway.org/grantees/sheena_sood_lta_17.

Vanissar Tarakali, www.vanissar.com.

Natalie Thoreson, www.invisionconsulting.org.

Evangeline Weiss, www.facebook.com/EvangelineFacilitates.

Kate Werning, www.katewerning.com.

Landon Whitsitt, www.landonwhitsitt.com.

92460968R00064

Made in the USA
Lexington, KY
05 July 2018